MANC
CITY F.C.

– THE 25 YEAR RECORD

1973 – 1998

SEASON BY SEASON WRITE-UPS
David Powter

EDITOR
Michael Robinson

CONTENTS

British Library Cataloguing in Publication Data
A catalogue record for this book is available from the British Library
ISBN 1-86223-025-0

Printed by Adlard Print & Typesetting Services, The Old School, The Green, Ruddington, Notts. NG11 6HH

MANCHESTER CITY
– Seasons 1973-74 to 1997-98

When the final whistle blew on 1997-98, the most turbulent period in Manchester City's history was completed with their first ever relegation to the third-flight. It was a most miserable conclusion to a rather muddled 25 years, yet for 19 of the seasons the men from Maine Road held top-flight status. It was a period when they won only one trophy (the League Cup, in 1976), but they were also close to winning the League Championship (in 1976-77) and the FA Cup (in 1981). In addition, three of the club's seven sorties into Europe were during this period. There was also, however, a remarkable lack of continuity in control of team affairs – over half the managerial appointments in the club's 111 year history were made during these 25 years, with a total of 16 men (excluding caretakers) in the managerial hot-seat during this period.

The last of these appointments was that of Joe Royle in February 1998. Sadly, the one time City centre-forward was unable to prevent a second relegation in three terms, despite a gallant 5-2 victory at Stoke on the last day of the season. City's away form was not really the problem in 1997-98, the real damage was done on Moss Side where 11 fixtures were lost, leaving some of the most loyal football supporters in the country in despair.

Twenty-five years previously, in the summer of 1973, Manchester City fans were not so much in despair but frustrated after their side had stuttered to 11th place in the First Division. Manager Malcolm Allison's spell in sole command had just ended. His surprise successor was Johnny Hart, the club's coach for ten years. Unfortunately, the loyal clubman Hart's reign was to be very brief. He resigned through ill-health in mid-November, with his side in mid-table, and was replaced by former Norwich City boss Ron Saunders. Tony Book hung up his boots (after 246 League appearances) to become the assistant-manager.

Despite a roll call that included the creative talent of Francis Lee, Denis Law, Rodney Marsh, Colin Bell and Mike Summerbee, City's 1973-74 form was indifferent with goals hard to come by. They netted just 37 times, Lee top scoring with ten – one more than Law. The latter's last was, of course, the infamous back-heel at Old Trafford, which sent his former team-mates down to the Second Division. City finished 14th, only four points above the relegation line.

Saunders was not at Maine Road to witness the end of the campaign, as he was sacked in mid-April and replaced by Book. The dour Saunders almost secured a trophy, though, when his side battled through to meet Wolves in the League Cup Final. The route to Wembley was a lengthy ten game affair, with a second replay needed to shake off Walsall and Maine Road replays required to kill off York City and Coventry City. In the semi-final plucky Plymouth Argyle's hopes were also destroyed at Maine Road, in the second leg, with Lee and Bell netting to make the aggregate score 3-1. Bell also scored at Wembley, but Wolves scored before and after to take the trophy. There was little joy for City in the FA Cup, with second-flight Nottingham Forest defeating them in the fourth round.

Late 1973-74 arrivals at Maine Road were the Sunderland pair of Denis Tueart and Micky Horswill. By the start of the following campaign, Book had also added ex-West Brom midfielder Asa Hartford to his squad which was by now shorn of Lee (who joined Derby County after netting 112 times in just 249 League appearances) and Law.

Book's side made a promising start to 1974-75, winning five of their first seven fixtures but despite heading the table briefly, in November, they lacked the consistency to take the title. Their home form was generally first class, losing just twice – against eventual Champions Derby and, ironically, to bottom boys Carlisle United. The main problem was on the road, where they won only twice. By finishing on an unbeaten four match run, City claimed eighth place, in a bunched finish, seven points behind the Champions. Full-back Glyn Pardoe made his 306th and last League appearance for City in 1974-75. Joe Royle, a mid-season purchase from Everton, took time to make his mark – scoring just once in 16 games. Bell was the main marksman, with 15 – one more than Tueart.

Tueart also scored 14 times in 1975-76 to be the top scorer as City finished eighth again. Failure to win more than twice on their travels once more hampered them. A 14 match unbeaten run prior to Christmas signalled something better, but they lost 11 of their final 20 fixtures to finish 17 points behind Champions Liverpool. Nevertheless, for the first time in six years, the Maine Road trophy-cabinet had to be unlocked after the League Cup was captured for the second time.

Norwich City (at the third attempt) and Nottingham Forest were both side-stepped to set up a fourth round derby with Manchester United at Maine Road. It was all over by half-time as City romped into a 3-0 lead. The final score was

4-0, with Tueart (2), Hartford and Royle scoring in front of an ecstatic 50,182 crowd. Book's side also hit four in two later League Cup matches at Maine Road. In the fifth round they disposed of Mansfield Town by a 4-2 scoreline to set up a two-legged semi-final with Middlesbrough. Jack Charlton's side held a 1-0 advantage from the first leg, but Ged Keegan, Alan Oakes, Peter Barnes and Royle were all on target, without reply, to send City back to the 'Twin Towers' for the second time in three seasons. Barnes struck again at Wembley, but it was Tueart who eventually broke Newcastle's hearts with a superb over-head kick to make the score 2-1.

The eleven who lifted City's last major honour on 28th February 1976 were: Joe Corrigan, Keegan, Willie Donachie, Mike Doyle, Dave Watson, Oakes, Barnes, Tommy Booth, Royle, Hartford and Tueart. Watson had arrived from Sunderland the previous June, a few days after Summerbee (357 League games – 46 goals) joined Burnley. Marsh had also departed, to Tampa Bay in January, while Bell missed the final through injury.

Another man on the move was Alan Oakes, who left for Chester City during the close season after a club record 565 League appearances. An important acquisition for 1976-77, though, was ex-Manchester United striker Brian Kidd (who signed from Arsenal). Bell missed the whole campaign through injury, but City finished in their highest position for nine seasons.

An unbeaten six match start lifted them to second place, before they hit a sticky patch which included a home reverse against Manchester United and a slip-up at Ipswich. However, those were the only two League defeats in the first 25 games, enabling City to sit in third spot behind Liverpool and Ipswich. Although Book's side later lost five times on the road (including the return with Manchester United and at Liverpool), they secured the runners-up spot in the final table. They finished with 56 points, just one behind Liverpool and four more than Ipswich. Kidd was the leading scorer with 21, three more than Tueart.

It was Kidd who had also scored City's only goal in the UEFA Cup, in 1976-77. His effort gave City a narrow success over Juventus in the first round first leg, but the Italians bounced back to score twice in Turin.

There was a promising start to the following campaign with England striker Mick Channon joining the squad. Book's side headed the table in early October after an unbeaten eight match start. They then stumbled badly to lose five of their next seven fixtures, but renewed their title challenge with six successive victories at the turn of the year and were still lying second in early March. However, they only won three of their last 13 games to finish 1977-78 in a disappointing fourth place – 12 points behind Champions Nottingham Forest. Kidd was again top scorer, with 16, while Channon and Tueart (who departed Maine Road in the February) netted 12 each. Royle's playing spell with the club had ended with his November move to Bristol City; but Bell returned from injury during the second half of the season. Barnes won his first England caps in 1977-78.

Manchester City's involvement in the UEFA Cup in 1977-78 was yet again brief. They were held 2-2 at home by Widzew Lodz in the first round and exited on away goals after a 0-0 draw in Poland.

A noticeable absentee in 1978-79 was Doyle (who won five England caps), who had moved to Stoke City after making 449 League appearances (32 goals) for Manchester City. His old club failed to win any of their first four fixtures, but improved to lie fifth at the end of October. However, they drifted badly with a dreadful run of 13 League matches without a win. In an attempt to improve matters Malcolm Allison returned in a coaching capacity, while Book's role became more general and Bill Taylor, who was the coach, left the club. Some improvement was detectable, but City still finished only 15th and suffered an embarrassing FA Cup defeat at the hands of Third Division Shrewsbury Town. Channon and Gary Owen were the joint top scorers, with 11 League goals.

The one ray of sunshine in 1978-79 was a much improved showing in Europe. A first half goal by Watson gave his side a boost in the opening match away to Twente. Although the Dutch outfit levelled on their own soil, it was City who progressed to UEFA Cup's second round with a 3-2 success at Maine Road. City then enjoyed a 4-0 triumph over Standard Liege and held on despite conceding two goals in the return leg. In the third round, goals by Kidd and Paul Power in a 2-2 away draw paved the way for a home triumph over AC Milan. Booth, Hartford and Kidd (who later in the campaign moved to Everton) found the net in the 3-0 win. Unfortunately, Borussia Mönchengladbach brought the excitement to an end in the quarter-final. The first leg ended 1-1 at Maine Road and the Germans eventually won through 4-2 on aggregate.

Allison's return ensured a number of changes in 1979-80. Sadly, the injury-jinxed Bell had to retire (394 League games – 117 goals), while Channon returned to Southampton. Barnes was sold to West Brom for a club record £748,000, the fee going towards the record £1,437,500 paid to Wolves for Steve

Daley. Other early season newcomers included Steve MacKenzie (from Crystal Palace), Michael Robinson (from Preston North End) and Yugoslav Dragoslav Stepanovic.

With so many new faces, City took time to gel, but they did force their way up to eighth by mid-October. That proved to be their seasonal peak before a dreadful 17 match post-Christmas spell saw them drop into relegation trouble. They only pulled clear by finishing the campaign with an eight match unbeaten run to take 17th place. Tueart returned to the club to play an important part in the end of term revival, as did £1 million signing Kevin Reeves on his arrival from Norwich. Robinson was the leading scorer with eight goals in 1979-80, a campaign that contained two undistinguished cup exits. City were knocked out of the League Cup by Second Division Sunderland and slid out of the FA Cup at Fourth Division Halifax Town.

Manchester City made a shocking start to 1980-81 and were rock bottom after failing to win any of their first 12 League games. They picked up significantly after John Bond arrived to replace the old managerial team of Book and Allison. Ten out of 15 matches were won as the Citizens lifted themselves into mid-table. Preoccupation with cup football cost them points later but City sill finished in a comfortable 12th position, with Reeves finishing as the top scorer, on the 12 goal mark. Bond strengthened the squad during the season with four signings – Bobby McDonald, Gerry Gow, Tommy Hutchison and Phil Boyer.

It was the two domestic cup competitions that really gave the Maine Road faithful something to cheer about in 1980-81. City reached the semi-final stage of the League Cup by defeating Stoke, Luton, Notts County and West Bromwich Albion. They eventually went out to Liverpool 2-1 on aggregate after losing the first leg at Maine Road by a single goal.

Bond's side went one better in the FA Cup, winning through to meet Spurs in the final. On the way they thrashed Allison's Crystal Palace (4-0) and Bond's old side Norwich (6-0). Peterborough were beaten narrowly at London Road, before Everton were knocked out in a quarter-final replay on Moss Side. McDonald netted twice and Power grabbed the other in the 3-1 success. Power was also on target as Ipswich were defeated in the semi-final at Villa Park.

Prospects of City's first FA Cup triumph for 12 years looked bright when Hutchison headed them in front just before the half-hour mark in the final. Sadly, Hutchison was also accredited with the Tottenham equaliser 11 minutes from time, when a Glenn Hoddle free-kick deflected off him and past Corrigan.

It was the first time for 35 years that a player had scored for both sides in the final.

The two teams returned to Wembley the following Thursday and this time it was the Londoners who took the lead, after seven minutes. However, MacKenzie soon levelled with a thunderous shot, and a foul on Dave Bennett just after the interval enabled Reeves to score from the spot to give City the initiative. It was not to be City's night though, with Spurs netting twice in the final 20 minutes to lift the trophy. Bond's gallant losers were: Corrigan, Ray Ranson, McDonald, Tommy Caton, Nicky Reid, Gow, Power, MacKenzie, Reeves, Bennett and Hutchison. Tony Henry appeared as a substitute in the first match, while Tueart came off the bench in the replay.

Stepanovic and Daley played their final games at Maine Road during 1980-81. Booth followed them out of the door the following October after making 382 League appearances for City. Gow also departed, but among those arriving in early 1981-82 were Trevor Francis (who was to move on again to Sampdoria for a club record £800,000 the following summer), Kevin Bond (the manager's son), Norwegian Åge Hareide and the returning Asa Hartford.

City made a mixed start to 1981-82, but picked up strongly to head the table in early January after a run of seven wins in nine matches. However, a dearth of goals in the last 17 games (of which only three were won) when they netted just nine times caused them to drift to finish tenth. Reeves was the top scorer with 13 – one more than Francis. There was no cup glory either with Second Division Barnsley knocking them out of the League Cup and Coventry ending their FA Cup hopes in the fourth round at Maine Road.

With David Cross arriving in the close season to lead the attack, City made a promising start to 1982-83 – winning seven of their first 13 fixtures to lie second in early November. However, Bond resigned in February after seeing his side win only three of their next 12 League games and make a disastrous 4-0 FA Cup exit at Brighton. When his assistant John Benson picked up the reins, City were comfortably placed in ninth place; however, City won only three more times and plummeted into trouble. They could – and should – have still saved themselves from relegation on the final day of the campaign when third bottom Luton were the visitors. A draw would have been enough to keep City up, but Luton stunned Maine Road with an 86th minute winner to leap-frog their hosts to safety. While the TV cameras captured the jubilant Hatters boss David Pleat racing across the turf, many hundreds in the Kippax wept silently as their club faced second-flight football for the first time in 17 years.

Despite the managerial change and subsequent relegation (in 20th place), City had a very settled side in 1982-83, with 12 men appearing at least 25 times. Cross top scored with 12 before moving on to Vancouver Whitecaps, while Corrigan was another to leave for North America before the end of the campaign after making 476 League appearances. Reeves (the second top scorer with seven) left at the end of the season to reunite with John Bond at Burnley. He was later joined at Turf Moor by several other ex-City players (including Donachie, Gow, Daley and Tueart).

Another man bound for Burnley was Benson, relegation costing him his job in Manchester. His successor was former Celtic boss Billy McNeill, who quickly brought in fellow Scots Derek Parlane and Jim Tolmie to boost the forward line. McNeill's side made an excellent start, winning 11 of their first 15 fixtures to lie second in mid-November. However, they failed to find the same consistency afterwards and by the end of February were chasing the top three. They only won four of their last 12 fixtures and finished fourth – one place and ten points short of the promotion line. Parlane was the main marksman with 16, three more than Tolmie. There was also further FA Cup humiliation in 1983-84, with City exiting to Fourth Division Blackpool.

McNeill's side made a sluggish start to 1984-85, winning only one of their first five fixtures. However, they defeated top-flight West Ham in the Milk Cup and a gradual improvement in the League saw them move into the top three in mid-January. Seven victories in eight games took them to the top of the table in March, but they then nearly threw away promotion by failing to win in six successive outings. They recovered to go into the final game with Charlton in third place on the same number of points as Portsmouth (who had a worse goal difference). City made no mistake, thumping the Londoners 5-1 at Maine Road to finish third on goal difference.

Three men were ever-present in McNeill's workmanlike 1984-85 side: keeper Alex Williams, David Phillips (who top scored with 12) and the popular Paul Power. Other important contributions came from Nicky Reid, Andy May, Steve Kinsey, Clive Wilson, Mick McCarthy, Graham Baker, Jim Melrose, Gordon Smith (second top scorer with 11) and Paul Simpson (who scored six vital goals in only nine starts).

City sat ninth in the early tables of 1985-86; but then went 11 matches without a win to slide into relegation trouble. However, they picked themselves up by winning nine of their next 13 fixtures to squeeze into the top half of the table. McNeill's side failed to win another game after 8th February – picking up just four points from a possible 39 – and were lucky not to finish lower than 15th, four points above the relegation line. Mark Lillis (a pre-season buy from Huddersfield Town) top scored with 11, two more than Gordon Davies (who had arrived from Chelsea).

The 1985-86 campaign did contain something for the City fans to cheer, however, with a FA Youth Cup final triumph over Manchester United (3-1 on aggregate). There was also a visit to Wembley for the final of the Full Members Cup. A crowd of 68,000 watched City lose an entertaining game 5-4 to Chelsea. Lillis (2), Kinsey and an own-goal were on the score-sheet for the Citizens.

McNeill left Maine Road to manage Aston Villa the following September, leaving his assistant Jimmy Frizzell holding the reins. Having won only one of the their first 12 fixtures, City were rock bottom at the end of November. Three successive victories raised their survival hopes, but a winless 14 match sequence in the new year eventually sank them. Frizzell's side were relegated in 21st place, with 39 points – five points short of the play-off spot. City netted just 36 times in 1986-87, with nine bagged by top scorer Imre Varadi.

By the start of 1987-88 Frizzell had stepped up to become general manager and Mel Machin was in charge of team affairs. City made another sluggish start and although they climbed to fourth place by mid-December they failed to deliver a meaningful promotion challenge. Their finishing position was ninth, 12 points short of a play-off place. Paul Stewart was the leading scorer, with 24, in front of Varadi (17) and David White (13). One highlight of the season saw Stewart, White and Tony Adcock all net hat-tricks in the 10-1 thrashing of Huddersfield, at Maine Road. Stewart, however, moved to Spurs during the following summer for a club record £1.7 million fee.

City reached the quarter-finals of both cup competitions in 1987-88. Top-flight Nottingham Forest and Watford were among their victims in the Littlewoods Cup. Everton eventually knocked them out 2-0 at Goodison Park, while their FA Cup run also came to a halt on Merseyside, when Liverpool beat them 4-0.

There was to be no FA Cup glory twelve months later when Third Division Brentford knocked them out in the fourth round. But instead Machin's men concentrated on winning promotion. They overcame a sticky start to climb to fourth at the halfway point. Six successive victories took them to the top of the table at the end of February; however, Chelsea motored past them to take the title by 17 points. In fact City's stuttering form in the latter part of the season – when they won only six of their last 16 fixtures – nearly cost them the other automatic promotion place. They just held off Crystal Palace's bid to claim the runners-up spot by one point. Trevor Morley's equaliser at Valley Parade on the last day of the season calmed the nerves and ignited the celebrations.

Paul Moulden was the 1988-89 top scorer with 13, one more than Morley. Other important contributions in City's most recent promotion campaign came from: Andy Dibble, Andy Hinchcliffe, Paul Lake, Ian Brightwell, Steve Redmond (the only ever present), Brian Gayle, Gary Megson, Wayne Biggins, Mark Seagraves, Neil McNab and David White.

Manchester City's return to the First Division proved to be a long season of struggle against relegation. The bright spot was a wonderful 5-1 thrashing of Manchester United but in contrast, six matches later, City suffered their heaviest defeat for 30 years when they went down 6-0 at Derby. The bad start cost Machin his job and instead, in early December, Howard Kendall moved into the managerial office with City bottom of the table. One of the new manager's first decisions was to buy Mark Ward from West Ham, with Morley and Ian Bishop going in the opposite direction. Kendall strengthened his squad further by bringing in Colin Hendry, Peter Reid, Niall Quinn, Adrian Heath, Wayne Clarke and Alan Harper. City lost only one of their last 11 fixtures to finish 14th, five points above the relegation line. Ten goal Clive Allen was the top scorer in 1989-90 – two more than White.

After losing their opening game of 1990-91, an unbeaten ten match run propelled City into the top five. So, it was a major disappointment when Kendall announced his resignation in early November to grasp a second opportunity to manage Everton. In his place Peter Reid took over in a player-manager role. City were very consistent for during the rest of the term, never falling below eighth and ended on a high note – with six victories in their last eight games – to take fifth place. It was the club's highest finish for 13 years. Quinn was the main marksman with 20, four more than White.

Although City won at Burnley and at Kendall's Everton, they faced FA Cup disappointment in 1990-91 when Second Division Notts County knocked them out in the fifth round. There was also cup disappointment in 1991-92, when Second Division Middlesbrough put them out of both competitions at Ayresome Park.

City were consistent in the League throughout 1991-92, with Reid able to field a very settled side. One of the most accomplished performers was Keith Curle (who went on to win three England caps), who had joined in the August for a club record £2.5 million from Wimbledon. Reid's side won their first three fixtures to head the early tables and later lost only once in 16 matches to keep tabs on the pacemakers. Their outside chance of snatching the title finally disappeared with a spell of five defeats in seven matches. Despite winning their last four games, they missed out on UEFA Cup qualification by five points in fifth place – 12 points behind Champions Leeds United. White headed the list of scorers with 18.

Twelve months later, 16 goal White (who was capped once by England) was also the leading scorer as a less consistent City finished ninth. Their final position in 1992-93 would have been far better but for a poor spell in the last two months when they won just twice in 11 outings. There was also major disappointment for Reid's side in the FA Cup when Spurs (who also knocked them out of the Coca-Cola Cup) defeated them 4-2 in a Maine Road quarter-final.

City make a disappointing start to the following campaign, collecting only one point from their first four fixtures. However, it was still a major surprise, though, when Reid was sacked on 24th September. Two days later Oxford United boss Brian Horton was appointed in his place. City gradually improved, but a spell of just one win in 16 fixtures left them in relegation trouble at the end of January. However, Horton's side lost only twice in the final third of the season to finish a nervous 16th, just three points above relegated Sheffield United. Goals were hard to come by in 1993-94, with six goal Mike Sheron top scoring – one more than both Quinn and Uwe Rösler (whose arrival from Dynamo Dresden boosted City in the final dozen games). The club also benefited from the return of Francis Lee in early 1994. The multi-millionaire former striker became chairman in succession to Peter Swales, who had held office for the previous 20 years.

There was to be disappointment for Manchester City in both cup competitions in 1993-94. Second-flight Nottingham Forest triumphed at Maine Road in a fourth round Coca-Cola Cup replay, while Second Division Cardiff City spun them out of the FA Cup.

Manchester City went one round further in the Coca-Cola Cup in 1994-95, before crashing out 4-0 at Crystal Palace. They enjoyed a healthy start to the League campaign, though, and, despite a 5-0 defeat at Old Trafford, nestled nicely in sixth place at the start of December. However, they only won four of their last 25 games and drifted to finish a disappointing 17th – just four points above the relegation line. Rösler was the leading scorer with 15, three more than Paul Walsh.

City's poor second half of the season cost Horton his job and during the summer Alan Ball left Southampton to take his place. His first signing was Georgiou Kinkladze for £2 million from Dynamo Tblisi. Also making their first appearances for City as 1995-96 opened were Kit Symons and keeper Eike Immel. Despite the new faces, City made a dreadful start, scrambling just two points from their first 11 fixtures – which included a run of eight successive defeats.

Matters only improved after Ball's side received a 6-0 thrashing at Anfield. A Nicky Summerbee strike provided the first League victory – over Bolton Wanderers – and the upturn in form saw ten points from the next four matches to move up to 15th place. Sadly, in the last of that unbeaten five match run – the 1-0 victory at Leeds – talented right-back Richard Edghill suffered an injury which curtailed his season.

Victories were more sporadic over the rest of the campaign, but Ball's side still went into the last five games with an even chance of avoiding relegation. They suffered two defeats, at home to Manchester United and at Wimbledon, but kept their hopes alive with 1-0 successes at home to Sheffield Wednesday and at Villa Park. This still left them in the third relegation berth, however, and their destiny was not in their own hands on the final day when Liverpool visited Maine Road. Nevertheless City could still have saved themselves if they had gained more points than any one of the three clubs immediately above them.

City's prospects looked bleak at half-time when a disinterested looking Liverpool led 2-0 but, urged on by a 31,436 crowd, Rösler and Symons managed to restore parity. However, with time running down, Ball mistakenly believed a point would be enough and urged his men to keep possession. This was a fatal error as the three clubs above actually all drew to leave City relegated and Maine Road awash with tears. Manchester City finished 18th with 38 points – the same total as Southampton and Coventry City but with an inferior goal difference. City netted only 33 League goals (never scoring more than two in the same match) in 1995-96, nine by top scorer Rösler.

Most of the blame for the relegation was directed at Ball and he resigned after just three games of 1996-97. Asa Hartford took over as caretaker while the board searched for the right man. Their choice was Steve Coppell who arrived on 7th October with City lying 14th and already out of the Coca-Cola Cup (5-1 on aggregate to Third Division Lincoln City). Coppell's reign lasted just 32 days before he resigned stating that the stress was too much for him. Coppell's assistant Phil Neal took over on a caretaker basis, with the side lying 17th. Neal's term of office ended in defeat at Barnsley, at the end of 1996, which left the club floundering with only three clubs below them. However, inspired by new manager Frank Clark, City embarked on a nine match unbeaten run. Although only four of the final 12 games ended in victory, City's extremely eventful 1996-97 campaign (containing five managers and 33 players) ended with them in 14th place. Rösler was the leading scorer with 15, three more than the skilful Kinkladze.

Clark's side were favourites to gain promotion from the First Division in the 1997-98 season; but the pundits could not have been much more wrong! Having failed to win any of their first four League games (and exiting the Coca-Cola Cup to Second Division Blackpool), City finally sparked to life with a 3-1 win at leaders Nottingham Forest. They posted their first home win with a 6-0 'Blue Moon' spanking of another of the early pacesetters Swindon Town, but significantly won only five more home games. By the time the board lost faith in Clark and replaced him with Joe Royle in mid-February, City were in dire straits – sitting just one off the bottom.

Another nail-biting run-in followed, climaxing in a final day visit to the Britannia Stadium, home of fellow strugglers Stoke City. On this occasion, Manchester City responded to the last day pressure and sent the Potters down with a 5-2 scoreline. But, cruelly, both the clubs immediately above the relegation line also won to push City into the third-flight for the first time in their history.

City finished in 22nd place, with 48 points – one point and one place short of safety. They only had themselves to blame, not winning more than two successive games and losing 11 home games. Paul Dickov was top scorer with nine goals, two more than Lee Bradbury. As many as 38 different players were used in 1997-98, a disastrous campaign that saw the last glimpses of Rösler and Kinkladze in light blue shirts and of Francis Lee in the boardroom. The next chapter in Manchester City's history can surely only be brighter. Certainly the Maine Road faithful deserve much better.

F.A. CUP

1973-74 SEASON
3rd Round
Jan 5 vs Oxford United (a) 5-2
Att: 13,435 Law 2, Summerbee 2, Marsh

4th Round
Jan 27 vs Nottingham Forest (a) 1-4
Att: 41,472 Carrodus

1974-75 SEASON
3rd Round (at Maine Road)
Jan 4 vs Newcastle United (a) 0-2
Att: 37,625

1975-76 SEASON
3rd Round
Jan 3 vs Hartlepool (h) 6-0
Att: 26,863 Oakes, Tueart 2 (1 pen), Booth 2, Hartford

4th Round
Jan 28 vs Stoke City (a) 0-1
Att: 38,072

1976-77 SEASON
3rd Round
Jan 8 vs West Bromwich Albion (h) 1-1
Att: 38,195 Kidd

Replay
Jan 11 vs West Bromwich Albion (a) 1-0
Att: 27,494 Royle

4th Round
Jan 29 vs Newcastle United (a) 3-1
Att: 45,300 Robertson 2 (1 pen), Woodcock

5th Round
Feb 26 vs Leeds United (a) 0-1
Att: 47,761

1977-78 SEASON
3rd Round
Jan 7 vs Leeds United (a) 2-1
Att: 38,517 Tueart, Barnes

4th Round
Jan 31 vs Nottingham Forest (a) 1-2
Att: 38,509 Kidd

1978-79 SEASON
3rd Round
Jan 15 vs Rotherham United (h) 0-0
Att: 26,029

Replay
Jan 17 vs Rotherham United (a) 4-2
Att: 13,758 Owen, Kidd 2, Barnes

4th Round
Jan 27 vs Shrewsbury Town (a) 0-2
Att: 14,215

1979-80 SEASON
3rd Round
Jan 5 vs Halifax Town (a) 0-1
Att: 12,599

1980-81 SEASON
3rd Round
Jan 3 vs Crystal Palace (h) 4-0
Att: 39,347 Reeves 2 (1 pen), Power, Boyer

4th Round
Jan 24 vs Norwich City (h) 6-0
Att: 38,919 Reeves, Gow, MacKenzie, Bennett, Power, McDonald

5th Round
Feb 14 vs Peterborough United (a) 1-0
Att: 27,780 Booth

6th Round
Mar 7 vs Everton (a) 2-2
Att: 52,791 Gow, Power

Replay
Mar 11 vs Everton (h) 3-1
Att: 52,532 McDonald 2, Power

Semi-Final (at Villa Park)
Apr 11 vs Ipswich Town 1-0 (aet)
Att: 46,537 Power

Final (at Wembley)
May 9 vs Tottenham Hotspur 1-1 (aet)
Att: 99,500 Hutchison

Replay (at Wembley)
May 14 vs Tottenham Hotspur 2-3
Att: 92,000 MacKenzie, Reeves (pen)

1981-82 SEASON
3rd Round
Jan 2 vs Cardiff City (h) 3-1
Att: 31,547 Francis 2, McDonald

4th Round
Jan 23 vs Coventry City (h) 1-3
Att: 31,276 Bond (pen)

1982-83 SEASON
3rd Round
Jan 8 vs Sunderland (a) 0-0
Att: 21,518

Replay
Jan 12 vs Sunderland (h) 2-1
Att: 22,356 Hartford, Cross

4th Round
Jan 29 vs Brighton & Hove Albion (a) 0-4
Att: 16,804

1983-84 SEASON
3rd Round
Jan 7 vs Blackpool (a) 1-2
Att: 15,377 Hetzke (own goal)

1984-85 SEASON
3rd Round
Jan 5 vs Coventry City (a) 1-2
Att: 15,643 Power

1985-86 SEASON
3rd Round
Jan 4 vs Walsall (a) 3-1
Att: 10,836 Davies, Simpson 2

4th Round
Jan 25 vs Watford (h) 1-1
Att: 31,632 Davies

Replay
Feb 3 vs Watford (a) 0-0
Att: 19,347

2nd Replay
Feb 6 vs Watford (h) 1-3
Att: 27,260 Kinsey

1986-87 SEASON
3rd Round
Jan 10 vs Manchester United (a) 0-1
Att: 54,294

1987-88 SEASON
3rd Round
Jan 9 vs Huddersfield Town (a) 2-2
Att: 18,102 Brightwell, Gidman

Replay
Jan 12 vs Huddersfield Town (h) 0-0
Att: 24,565

2nd Replay
Jan 25 vs Huddersfield Town (a) 3-0
Att: 21,510 Hinchcliffe, White, Varadi

4th Round
Jan 30 vs Blackpool (a) 1-1
Att: 10,835 Lake

Replay
Feb 3 vs Blackpool (h) 2-1
Att: 26,503 Stewart, Simpson

5th Round
Feb 20 vs Plymouth Argyle (h) 3-1
Att: 29,206 Scott, Simpson, Moulden

6th Round
Mar 13 vs Liverpool (h) 0-4
Att: 44,047

1988-89 SEASON
3rd Round
Jan 7 vs Leicester City (h) 1-0
Att: 23,838 McNab (pen)

4th Round
Jan 28 vs Brentford (a) 1-3
Att: 12,100 Gleghorn

1989-90 SEASON
3rd Round
Jan 6 vs Millwall (h) 0-0
Att: 25,038

Replay
Jan 9 vs Millwall (a) 1-1 (aet)
Att: 17,696 Hendry

2nd Replay
Jan 15 vs Millwall (a) 1-3
Att: 17,771 Lake

1990-91 SEASON
3rd Round
Jan 6 vs Burnley (a) 1-0
Att: 20,331 Hendry

4th Round
Jan 26 vs Port Vale (a) 2-1
Att: 19,132 Quinn, Allen

5th Round
Feb 16 vs Notts County (a) 0-1
Att: 18,979

1991-92 SEASON
3rd Round
Jan 4 vs Middlesbrough (a) 1-2
Att: 21,174 Reid

1992-93 SEASON
3rd Round
Jan 2 vs Reading (h) 1-1
Att: 20,523 Sheron

Replay
Jan 13 vs Reading (a) 4-0
Att: 15,065 Sheron, Holden, Flitcroft, Quinn

4th Round
Jan 23 vs Queen's Park Rangers (a) 2-1
Att: 18,655 White, Vonk

5th Round
Feb 13 vs Barnsley (h) 2-0
Att: 32,807 White 2

6th Round
Mar 7 vs Tottenham Hotspur (h) 2-4
Att: 23,050 Sheron, Phelan

1993-94 SEASON
3rd Round
Jan 8 vs Leicester City (h) 4-1
Att: 22,613 Ingebritsen 3, Kernaghan

4th Round
Jan 29 vs Cardiff City (a) 0-1
Att: 20,486

1994-95 SEASON
3rd Round
Jan 8 vs Notts County (a) 2-2
Att: 12,376 Beagrie, Brightwell D

Replay
Jan 18 vs Notts County (h) 5-2
Att: 14,261 Rosler 4, Gaudino

4th Round
Jan 28 vs Aston Villa (h) 1-0
Att: 21,177 Walsh

5th Round
Feb 19 vs Newcastle United (a) 1-3
Att: 33,219 Rosler

1995-96 SEASON
3rd Round
Jan 6 vs Leicester City (a) 0-0
Att: 20,640

Replay
Jan 17 vs Leicester City (h) 5-0
Att: 19,980 Rosler, Kinkladze, Quinn, Lomas, Creaney

4th Round
Feb 7 vs Coventry City (a) 2-2
Att: 18,709 Busst (own goal), Flitcroft

Replay
Feb 14 vs Coventry City (h) 2-1
Att: 22,419 Clough, Quinn

5th Round
Feb 18 vs Manchester United (a) 1-2
Att: 42,692 Rosler

1996-97 SEASON

3rd Round
Jan 25 vs Brentford (a) 1-0
Att: 12,019 Summerbee

4th Round
Feb 5 vs Watford (h) 3-1
Att: 24,031 Heaney, Summerbee, Rosler

5th Round
Feb 15 vs Middlesbrough (h) 0-1
Att: 30,462

1997-98 SEASON

3rd Round
Jan 3 vs Bradford City (h) 2-0
Att: 23,686 Rosler, Brown

4th Round
Jan 25 vs West Ham United (h) 1-2
Att: 26,495 Kinkladze

LEAGUE CUP

1973-74 SEASON

2nd Round
Oct 2 vs Walsall (a) 0-0
Att: 12,943

Replay
Oct 22 vs Walsall (h) 0-0
Att: 19,428

2nd Replay
Oct 30 vs Walsall (h) 4-0
Att: 13,646 Lee 3 (2 pens), Bell

3rd Round
Nov 6 vs Carlisle United (a) 1-0
Att: 14,472 Lee

4th Round
Nov 21 vs York City (a) 0-0
Att: 15,360

Replay
Dec 5 vs York City (h) 4-1
Att: 17,972 Marsh 3, Lee (pen)

5th Round
Dec 19 vs Coventry City (a) 2-2
Att: 12,661 Booth, Leman

Replay
Jan 16 vs Coventry City (h) 4-2
Att: 25,409 Summerbee, Lee 2 (1 pen)

Semi-Final (1st leg)
Jan 23 vs Plymouth Argyle (a) 1-1
Att: 30,390 Booth

Semi-Final (2nd leg)
Jan 30 vs Plymouth Argyle (h) 2-0
Att: 40,117 Lee, Bell

Final (at Wembley)
Mar 2 vs Wolverhampton Wanderers 1-2
Att: 100,000 Bell

1974-75 SEASON

2nd Round
Sep 10 vs Scunthorpe United (h) 6-0
Att: 14,790 Bell 3, Doyle, Marsh, Barrett

3rd Round
Oct 9 vs Manchester United (a) 0-1
Att: 55,225

1975-76 SEASON

2nd Round
Sep 10 vs Norwich City (a) 1-1
Att: 18,332 Watson

Replay
Sep 17 vs Norwich City (h) 2-2 (aet)
Att: 29,667 Royle, Tueart (pen)

2nd Replay
Sep 29 vs Norwich City (h) 6-1
Att: 6,238 Tueart 3 (2 pens), Royle, Butler (own goal), Doyle

3rd Round
Oct 8 vs Nottingham Forest (h) 2-1
Att: 26,536 Royle, Bell

4th Round
Nov 12 vs Manchester United (h) 4-0
Att: 50,182 Tueart 2, Hartford, Royle

5th Round
Dec 3 vs Mansfield Town (h) 4-2
Att: 30,022 Royle, Oakes, Tueart, Hartford

Semi-Final (1st leg)
Jan 13 vs Middlesbrough (a) 0-1
Att: 35,000

Semi-Final (2nd leg)
Jan 21 vs Middlesbrough (h) 4-0
Att: 44,426 Keegan, Oakes, Barnes, Royle

Final (at Wembley)
Feb 28 vs Newcastle United 2-1
Att: 100,000 Barnes, Tueart

1976-77 SEASON

2nd Round
Sep 1 vs Aston Villa (a) 0-3
Att: 34,585

1977-78 SEASON

2nd Round
Aug 31 vs Chesterfield (a) 1-0
Att: 17,500 Kidd

3rd Round
Oct 25 vs Luton Town (a) 1-1
Att: 16,443 Barnes

Replay
Nov 1 vs Luton Town (h) 0-0
Att: 28,254

2nd Replay
Nov 9 vs Luton Town (h) 3-2
Att: 13,043 Tueart (pen), Channon, Kidd

4th Round
Nov 29 vs Ipswich Town (a) 2-1
Att: 22,645 Kidd, Tueart

5th Round
Jan 18 vs Arsenal (h) 0-0
Att: 42,000

Replay
Jan 24 vs Arsenal (a) 0-1
Att: 57,748

1978-79 SEASON

2nd Round
Aug 29 vs Grimsby Town (h) 2-0
Att: 21,481 Moore (own goal), Palmer

3rd Round
Oct 4 vs Blackpool (a) 1-1
Att: 18,868 Channon

Replay
Aug 10 vs Blackpool (h) 3-0
Att: 26,213 Owen 2 (1 pen), Booth

4th Round
Nov 8 vs Norwich City (a) 3-1
Att: 19,413 Barnes, Channon 2

5th Round
Dec 12 vs Southampton (a) 1-2
Att: 21,500 Nicholl (own goal)

1979-80 SEASON

2nd Round (1st leg)
Aug 28 vs Sheffield Wednesday (a) 1-1
Att: 15,000 Viljoen

2nd Round (2nd leg)
Sep 4 vs Sheff. Wednesday (h) 2-1 (agg. 3-2)
Att: 24,074 Henry 2

3rd Round
Sep 26 vs Sunderland (h) 1-1
Att: 26,181 Robinson

Replay
Oct 3 vs Sunderland (a) 0-1
Att: 33,559

1980-81 SEASON

2nd Round (1st leg)
Aug 27 vs Stoke City (a) 1-1
Att: 13,176 Henry

2nd Round (2nd leg)
Sep 3 vs Stoke City (h) 3-0 (agg. 4-1)
Att: 21,356 Henry, Bennett 2

3rd Round
Sep 23 vs Luton Town (a) 2-1
Att: 10,030 Bennett, Henry

4th Round
Oct 29 vs Notts County (h) 5-1
Att: 26,363 Tueart 4, Bennett

5th Round
Dec 3 vs West Bromwich Albion (h) 2-1
Att: 35,011 Bennett, Henry

Semi-Final (1st leg)
Jan 14 vs Liverpool (h) 0-1
Att: 48,045

Semi-Final (2nd leg)
Feb 10 vs Liverpool (a) 1-1 (agg. 1-2)
Att: 46,711 Reeves

1981-82 SEASON

2nd Round (1st leg)
Oct 7 vs Stoke City (h) 2-0
Att: 23,146 Smith (own goal), Hartford

2nd Round (2nd leg)
Oct 28 vs Stoke City (a) 0-2 (aet)(agg. 2-2)
Att: 17,373
Manchester City won 9-8 on penalties

3rd Round
Nov 11 vs Northampton Town (h) 3-1
Att: 21,139 McDonald, Tueart 2

4th Round
Dec 2 vs Barnsley (a) 0-1
Att: 33,792

1982-83 SEASON

2nd Round (1st leg)
Oct 5 vs Wigan Athletic (a) 1-1
Att: 12,194 Tueart

2nd Round (2nd leg)
Oct 27 vs Wigan Athletic (h) 2-0
Att: 16,083 Power 2

3rd Round
Nov 10 vs Southampton (h) 1-1
Att: 17,463 Tueart (pen)

Replay
Nov 24 vs Southampton (a) 0-4
Att: 13,298

1983-84 SEASON

2nd Round (1st leg)
Oct 5 vs Torquay United (a) 0-0
Att: 6,439

2nd Round (2nd leg)
Oct 25 vs Torquay United (h) 6-0 (agg. 6-0)
Att: 14,021 Tolmie 2 (1 pen), Parlane 3, Hoyland

3rd Round
Nov 9 vs Aston Villa (a) 0-3
Att: 23,922

1984-85 SEASON

2nd Round (1st leg)
Sep 25 vs Blackpool (h) 4-2
Att: 13,344 Wilson, Cunningham 2, McCarthy

2nd Round (2nd leg)
Oct 9 vs Blackpool (a) 3-1 (agg. 7-3)
Att: 10,966 Smith, Tolmie 2

3rd Round
Oct 31 vs West Ham United (h) 0-0
Att: 20,510

Replay
Nov 6 vs West Ham United (a) 2-1
Att: 17,461 Cunningham, Kinsey

4th Round
Nov 12 vs Chelsea (a) 1-4
Att: 26,364 Smith

1985-86 SEASON

2nd Round (1st leg)
Sep 25 vs Bury (a) 2-1
Att: 11,377 Melrose, Wilson

2nd Round (2nd leg)
Oct 8 vs Bury (h) 2-1 (agg. 4-2)
Att: 9,799 Melrose, Lillis

3rd Round
Oct 30 vs Arsenal (h) 1-2
Att: 18,279 Davies

1986-87 SEASON

2nd Round (1st leg)
Sep 23 vs Southend United (a) 0-0
Att: 6,182

2nd Round (2nd leg)
Oct 8 vs Southend United (h) 2-1 (agg. 2-1)
Att: 9,373 Simpson, McNab

3rd Round
Oct 28 vs Arsenal (a) 1-3
Att: 21,604 Simpson

1987-88 SEASON

2nd Round (1st leg)
Sep 22 vs Wolverhampton Wands. (h) 1-2
Att: 8,551 Adcock

2nd Round (2nd leg)
Oct 6 vs Wolverhampton (a) 2-0 (agg. 3-2)
Att: 13,843 Hinchcliffe, Gidman

3rd Round
Oct 27 vs Nottingham Forest (h) 3-0
Att: 15,168 Varadi 2, Stewart

4th Round
Nov 17 vs Watford (h) 3-1
Att: 20,357 White 2, Stewart

5th Round
Jan 20 vs Everton (a) 0-2
Att: 40,014

1988-89 SEASON

2nd Round (1st leg)
Sep 18 vs Plymouth Argyle (h) 1-0
Att: 9,454 White

2nd Round (2nd leg)
Oct 12 vs Plymouth Argyle (a) 6-3 (agg. 7-3)
Att: 8,794 Biggins, Gleghorn 2, Moulden, McNab (pen), Lake

3rd Round
Nov 2 vs Sheffield United (h) 4-2
Att: 16,609 Moulden 3, Morley

4th Round
Nov 29 vs Luton Town (a) 1-3
Att: 10,178 White

1989-90 SEASON

2nd Round (1st leg)
Sep 19 vs Brentford (a) 1-2
Att: 6,065 Oldfield

2nd Round (2nd leg)
Oct 4 vs Brentford (h) 4-1 (agg. 5-3)
Att: 17,874 White, Morley 2, Oldfield

3rd Round
Oct 25 vs Norwich City (h) 3-1
Att: 20,126 White, Bishop, Allen

4th Round
Nov 22 vs Coventry City (h) 0-1
Att: 23,355

1990-91 SEASON

2nd Round (1st leg)
Sep 26 vs Torquay United (a) 4-0
Att: 5,249 Hendry, Allen, Harper, Beckford

2nd Round (2nd leg)
Oct 10 vs Torquay United (h) 0-0 (agg. 4-0)
Att: 12,204

3rd Round
Oct 30 vs Arsenal (h) 1-2
Att: 26,825 Allen

1991-92 SEASON

2nd Round (1st leg)
Sep 25 vs Chester City (h) 3-1
Att: 10,987 White 2, Quinn

2nd Round (2nd leg)
Oct 8 vs Chester City (a) 3-0 (agg. 6-1)
Att: 4,146 Allen, Sheron, Brennan

3rd Round
Oct 29 vs Queen's Park Rangers (h) 0-0
Att: 15,512

Replay
Nov 20 vs Queen's Park Rangers (a) 3-1
Att: 11,033 Heath 2, Quinn

4th Round
Dec 4 vs Middlesbrough (a) 1-2
Att: 17,286 White

1992-93 SEASON

2nd Round (1st leg)
Sep 23 vs Bristol Rovers (h) 0-0
Att: 9,967

2nd Round (2nd leg)
Oct 7 vs Bristol Rovers (a) 2-1
Att: 7,823 Maddison (own goal), Holden

3rd Round
Oct 28 vs Tottenham Hotspur (h) 0-1
Att: 18,399

1993-94 SEASON

2nd Round (1st leg)
Sep 22 vs Reading (h) 1-1
Att: 9,280 White

2nd Round (2nd leg)
Oct 6 vs Reading (a) 2-1 (agg. 3-2)
Att: 10,052 Lomas, Quinn

3rd Round
Oct 26 vs Chelsea (h) 1-0
Att: 16,713 White

4th Round
Dec 1 vs Nottingham Forest (a) 0-0
Att: 22,195

Replay
Dec 15 vs Nottingham Forest (h) 1-2
Att: 14,117 Vonk

1994-95 SEASON

2nd Round (1st leg)
Sep 20 vs Barnet (a) 0-1
Att: 3,120

2nd Round (2nd leg)
Oct 5 vs Barnet (h) 4-1 (agg. 4-2)
Att: 11,545 Quinn 2, Walsh, Summerbee

3rd Round
Oct 25 vs Queen's Park Rangers (a) 4-3
Att: 11,701 Summerbee, Curle (pen), Beagrie, Lomas

4th Round
Nov 30 vs Newcastle United (h) 1-1
Att: 25,162 Rosler

Replay
Dec 21 vs Newcastle United (a) 2-0
Att: 30,156 Rosler, Walsh

5th Round
Jan 11 vs Crystal Palace (a) 0-4
Att: 16,668

1995-96 SEASON

2nd Round (1st leg)
Sep 19 vs Wycombe Wanderers (a) 0-0
Att: 7,443

2nd Round (2nd leg)
Oct 4 vs Wycombe Wands. (h) 4-0 (agg. 4-0)
Att: 11,474 Rosler 2, Quinn, Curle (pen)

3rd Round
Oct 25 vs Liverpool (a) 0-4
Att: 29,394

1996-97 SEASON

2nd Round (1st leg)
Sep 17 vs Lincoln City (a) 1-4
Att: 7,599 Rosler

2nd Round (2nd leg)
Sep 24 vs Lincoln City (h) 0-1 (agg. 1-5)
Att: 14,242

1997-98 SEASON

1st Round (1st leg)
Aug 11 vs Blackpool (a) 0-1
Att: 8,084

2nd Round (2nd leg)
Aug 26 vs Blackpool (h) 1-0 (aet)(agg. 1-1)
Att: 12,563 Horlock
Blackpool won 4-2 on penalties

UEFA CUP

1976-77 SEASON

1st Round (1st leg)
Sep 15 vs Juventus (h) 1-0
Att: 36,955 Kidd

1st Round (2nd leg)
Sep 29 vs Juventus (a) 0-2 (agg. 1-2)
Att: 55,000

1977-78 SEASON

1st Round (1st leg)
Sep 14 vs Widzew Lodz (h) 2-2
Att: 33,695 Barnes, Channon

1st Round (2nd leg)
Sep 28 vs Widzew Lodz (a) 0-0 (agg. 2-2)
Att: 40,000
Widzew Lodz won on away goals

1978-79 SEASON

1st Round (1st leg)
Sep 13 vs FC Twente (a) 1-1
Att: 12,000 Watson

1st Round (2nd leg)
Sep 27 vs FC Twente (h) 3-2 (agg. 4-3)
Att: 29,330 Wildschut (own goal), Kidd, Bell

2nd Round (1st leg)
Oct 18 vs Standard Liege (h) 4-0
Att: 27,489 Hartford, Kidd 2 (1 pen), Palmer

2nd Round (2nd leg)
Nov 1 vs Standard Liege (a) 0-2 (agg. 4-2)
Att: 30,000

3rd Round (1st leg)
Nov 23 vs AC Milan (a) 2-2
Att: 40,000 Kidd, Power

3rd Round (2nd leg)
Dec 6 vs AC Milan (h) 3-0 (agg. 5-2)
Att: 38,026 Booth, Hartford, Kidd

Quarter-Final (1st leg)
Mar 7 vs Borussia Mönchengladbach (h) 1-1
Att: 39,005 Channon

Quarter-Final (2nd leg)
Mar 20 vs Bor. Mönchengl. (a) 1-3 (agg. 2-4)
Att: 35,000 Deyna

1973-74

1	Aug	25	(h)	Birmingham C	W	3-1	Law 2, Bell	34,178
2		29	(a)	Derby Co	L	0-1		31,295
3	Sep	1	(a)	Stoke C	D	1-1	Law	22,434
4		5	(h)	Coventry C	W	1-0	Marsh (pen)	30,931
5		8	(h)	Norwich C	W	2-1	Bell, Lee	31,209
6		11	(a)	Coventry C	L	1-2	Marsh	27,394
7		15	(a)	Leicester C	D	1-1	Bell	28,466
8		22	(h)	Chelsea	W	3-2	Towers, Lee 2 (1 pen)	32,118
9		29	(a)	Burnley	L	0-3		24,492
10	Oct	6	(h)	Southampton	D	1-1	Marsh	27,727
11		13	(a)	Newcastle U	L	0-1		35,025
12		20	(a)	Sheffield U	W	2-1	Law, Dearden (og)	25,234
13		27	(h)	Leeds U	L	0-1		45,346
14	Nov	3	(a)	Wolverhampton W	D	0-0		21,499
15		10	(h)	Arsenal	L	1-2	Lee	31,041
16		17	(h)	Q.P.R.	W	1-0	Lee (pen)	30,486
17		24	(a)	Ipswich T	L	1-2	Leman	19,143
18	Dec	8	(a)	West Ham U	L	1-2	Lee	20,790
19		15	(a)	Tottenham H	W	2-0	Booth, Bell	17,066
20		22	(h)	Burnley	W	2-0	Bell, Doyle	28,114
21		26	(a)	Everton	L	0-2		36,007
22		29	(a)	Norwich C	D	1-1	Law	24,303
23	Jan	1	(h)	Stoke C	D	0-0		35,009
24		12	(h)	Leicester C	W	2-0	Law, Marsh	27,488
25		19	(a)	Birmingham C	D	1-1	Law	31,401
26	Feb	2	(h)	Tottenham H	D	0-0		24,652
27		6	(h)	Derby Co	W	1-0	Bell	22,845
28		9	(a)	Chelsea	L	0-1		20,206
29		23	(a)	Southampton	W	2-0	Marsh, Law	19,234
30	Mar	9	(a)	Leeds U	L	0-1		36,578
31		13	(h)	Manchester U	D	0-0		51,331
32		16	(h)	Sheffield U	L	0-1		26,220
33		23	(a)	Arsenal	L	0-2		25,319
34		27	(h)	Newcastle U	W	2-1	Lee 2	21,590
35		30	(h)	Wolverhampton W	D	1-1	Lee	25,236
36	Apr	2	(h)	Everton	D	1-1	Tueart	22,918
37		6	(h)	Ipswich T	L	1-3	Summerbee	22,269
38		9	(a)	Q.P.R.	L	0-3		20,461
39		12	(h)	Liverpool	D	1-1	Lee	43,248
40		16	(a)	Liverpool	L	0-4		50,781
41		20	(h)	West Ham U	W	2-1	Booth, Bell	29,700
42		27	(a)	Manchester U	W	1-0	Law	56,966

FINAL LEAGUE POSITION: 14th in Division One

Appearances

Sub. Appearances

Goals

Corrigan	Book	Donachie	Doyle	Booth	Oakes	Summerbee	Bell	Law	Lee	Marsh	Carrodus	Pardoe	Towers	Healey	Whelan	Leman	MacRae	Lester	Barrett	Daniels	Horswill	Tueart	Henson	
1	2*	3	4	5	6	7	8	9	10	11	12													1
1		3	4	5	6	7	8	9	10	11		2												2
1		3	4	5	6	7	8	9	10*	11	12	2												3
1		3	4	5	6*	7	8	9	12	11	10	2												4
1		3	4	5		7	8	9*	10	11	12	2	6											5
1		3	4	5		7	8		10	11	9	2	6											6
1	2	3	4	5	6	7	8		10	11			9											7
1	2	3	4	5	6	7	8		10	9			11											8
1	2	3	4	5	6	7	8		10	9			11											9
		3	4*	5	6	7	8			11		2	9	1	12	10								10
		3	4	5	6	7	8	9	10	12		2	11*	1										11
		3	4	5	6	7	8	9	10	11		2					1							12
		3	4	5	6	7	8	9*	10			2	11			12	1							13
		3	4*	5	6	11	8	12	9		7	2	10				1							14
		3		5	6*	7	8	9	10		11	2				12	1	4						15
		3		5		7	8	9	10	11		2	6				1		4					16
		3	4	5		9	8			11		2	6			10	1		7					17
		3	4	5		7	8		9	11		2	6			10	1							18
		3	4	5		7	8	10		9		2*	6			11	1		12					19
		3	4	5		7	8		10	9		2	6			11	1							20
		3	4	5		7	8	12	10	9		2	6			11*	1							21
		3	4	5			8	10		9	7		6			11	1		2					22
1		3	4	5		7	8	10		9			6			11			2					23
		3	4	5		7	8	9*	10	11			6			12	1		2					24
		3	4	5		7	8	10	9	11		12	6*				1		2					25
		3	4	5	10		8				11	7	6			9	1		2					26
		3	4	5	10		8				11	7	6				1		2	9				27
		3	4	5	6	7	8				11	10	12				1		2	9*				28
		3	4	5		7	8	10		11	9	2	6				1							29
1		3	4	5		7	8	10	9	11		2	6											30
1		3	4	5	10	7	8				9	2									6	11		31
1		3	4	5	10	7	8				9*					12			2		6	11		32
		3	4	5	10	7	8		9			2					1				6	11		33
		3	4	5	10	7	8		9			2			12		1				6*	11		34
		3	6	5	10	7	8		9		11	2					1				4			35
		3	4		10	7			9*		8	2			12		1		5		6	11		36
		3	4		10	7	8				9	2					1		5		6	11		37
		3	4*	5	6	7	8	10	9		11	2					1				12			38
		3		5	6	7	8	10	9		11	2					1		4					39
		3	4	5	6	7	8	10*	9			2					1		11	12				40
1		3	4	5	6	7	8	10	9										2			11		41
1		3	4	5	6	7	8	10*	9										2			11	12	42
15	4	42	39	40	28	39	41	22	29	23	16	31	23	2		9	25	1	16	2	7	8		
								2	1	1	3	1	1		3	4			1	1	1		1	
			1	2		1	7	9	10	5			1			1						1		

1974-75

1	Aug	17	(h)	West Ham U	W 4-0	Tueart, Marsh 2, Doyle	30,240
2		21	(h)	Tottenham H	W 1-0	Hartford	31,549
3		24	(a)	Arsenal	L 0-4		27,143
4		28	(a)	Tottenham H	W 2-1	Bell, Booth	20,079
5		31	(h)	Leeds U	W 2-1	Summerbee, Bell	37,919
6	Sep	7	(a)	Coventry C	D 2-2	Marsh, Oakes	15,440
7		14	(h)	Liverpool	W 2-0	Marsh, Tueart	45,194
8		21	(a)	Middlesbrough	L 0-3		30,256
9		24	(a)	Carlisle U	D 0-0		17,900
10		28	(h)	Q.P.R.	W 1-0	Marsh	30,647
11	Oct	5	(h)	Chelsea	D 1-1	Bell	32,412
12		12	(a)	Burnley	L 1-2	Tueart (pen)	23,406
13		16	(h)	Arsenal	W 2-1	Tueart 2	26,658
14		19	(h)	Luton T	W 1-0	Summerbee	30,649
15		26	(a)	Ipswich T	D 1-1	Bell	25,171
16	Nov	2	(a)	Everton	L 0-2		43,905
17		9	(h)	Stoke C	W 1-0	Marsh	36,966
18		16	(a)	Birmingham C	L 0-4		35,143
19		23	(h)	Leicester C	W 4-1	Tueart, Daniels 2, Bell	31,628
20		30	(a)	Newcastle U	L 1-2	Marsh	37,600
21	Dec	7	(h)	Sheffield U	W 3-2	Hammond, Bell, Marsh	29,675
22		14	(a)	West Ham U	D 0-0		33,908
23		21	(h)	Wolverhampton W	D 0-0		29,326
24		26	(a)	Liverpool	L 1-4	Bell	46,062
25		28	(h)	Derby Co	L 1-2	Bell	40,188
26	Jan	11	(a)	Sheffield U	D 1-1	Booth	25,190
27		18	(h)	Newcastle U	W 5-1	Hammond, Tueart 3 (1 pen), Bell	32,021
28	Feb	1	(a)	Stoke C	L 0-4		32,007
29		8	(h)	Everton	W 2-1	Bell, Tueart	44,718
30		22	(h)	Birmingham C	W 3-1	Royle, Tueart, Bell	33,240
31	Mar	1	(a)	Leeds U	D 2-2	Oakes, Donachie	47,489
32		8	(a)	Leicester C	L 0-1		23,059
33		15	(a)	Q.P.R.	L 0-2		22,102
34		19	(h)	Carlisle U	L 1-2	Barnes	24,047
35		22	(h)	Coventry C	W 1-0	Tueart (pen)	25,903
36		28	(h)	Middlesbrough	W 2-1	Marsh, Bell	37,772
37		29	(a)	Wolverhampton W	L 0-1		21,716
38	Apr	1	(a)	Derby Co	L 1-2	Bell	32,966
39		12	(a)	Chelsea	W 1-0	Hartford	26,249
40		19	(h)	Burnley	W 2-0	Bell, Tueart	30,723
41		23	(h)	Ipswich T	D 1-1	Bell	29,391
42		26	(a)	Luton T	D 1-1	Tueart	20,768

FINAL LEAGUE POSITION: 8th in Division One

Appearances

Sub. Appearances

Goals

MacRae	Barrett	Donachie	Doyle	Clarke	Oakes	Henson	Bell	Marsh	Hartford	Tueart	Booth	Summerbee	Hammond	Pardoe	Horswill	Barnes	Leman	Daniels	Corrigan	Royle	Keegan	
1	2	3	4	5	6	7	8	9	10	11												1
1	2	3	4	5	6	7	8	9	10	11												2
1	2	3	4	5	6	7	8	9	10	11												3
1	2	3	4		6		8	9	10	11	5	7										4
1	2	3	4		6		8	9	10	11	5	7										5
1	2	3	4		6		8	9	10	11	5	7										6
1	2	3	4	5	6	12	8	9*	10	11		7										7
1	2	3	4	5	6		8	9	10	11		7										8
1	5	3	4*		6	12	8	9	10	11		7	2									9
1	5	3	4		6		8	9	10	11		7	2									10
1	5*		4		6		8	9	10	11		7	2	3	12							11
1			4	5	6	10	8			9		7	2	3		11					2	12
1		3	4	5	6	10	8	9		11*		7	2				12					13
1		3	4	5	6	10	8	9				7	2			11						14
1	11	3	4	5	6	10	8	9				7	2									15
1	11	3	4	5	6	12	8	9	10			7	2*									16
1	5	3	4		6		8	9	10	11		7	2									17
1	5	3	4		6	10	8	9		11		7	2									18
1		3	5		6	8	4	9	10	11			2					7				19
1	12	3	5		6	8	4	9	10	11			2*					7				20
1		3	5		6	4	8	9	10	11*		12	2					7				21
1		3	5*		6	4	8	9	10	11			2		7			12				22
	2	3	4	5			8	9	10	11					6			7	1			23
		3	6	5			4	9	10	11		7			2				1	8		24
		3	5		6		4	9	10	11			2		7				1	8		25
		3	4		6		8	9		11	5	7	2						1	10		26
		3	4		6		8	9		11	5	7	2						1	10		27
1		3	4		6		8		10	11	5	7	2							9		28
1		2	4		6		8	9		11	5*	7		3	12					10		29
1		2	4		6		8	9		11	5	7		3						10		30
1		2	4		6		8	9		11	5	7		3						10		31
1		2	4*		6		8	9	12	11	5	7		3						10		32
		2	4		3		8	9	6	11	5	7							1	10		33
		3	2	5	6		8		4	11		7*				10			1	9	12	34
		3	4		6		10			11	5	7	2						1	9	8	35
		3	4		6		8	9		11	5		2						1	10	7	36
	4	3	5		6		8		10	11			2					12	1	9	7*	37
		3	4		6		8	9	7	11	5		2						1	10		38
		3	4		6		8	9	7	11	5		2					12	1	10*		39
		3	4		6		8	9	7	11	5		2					10	1			40
		3	4		6		8	9	7	11	5		2					10	1			41
		3	4		6		8	9*	7	11	5		2					10	1		12	42
27	17	40	42	13	40	12	42	37	29	39	18	26	26	6	4	3		7	15	16	3	
	1					3			1			1			2		1	3			2	
		1	1		2		15	9	2	14	2	2	2			1		2		1		

1975-76

1	Aug	16	(h)	Norwich C	W	3-0	Bell, Tueart 2	29,103
2		20	(h)	Leicester C	D	1-1	Birchenall (og)	28,557
3		23	(a)	Coventry C	L	0-2		21,097
4		27	(a)	Aston Villa	L	0-1		35,212
5		30	(h)	Newcastle U	W	4-0	Tueart 2 (2 pens), Royle 2	31,875
6	Sep	6	(a)	West Ham U	L	0-1		29,752
7		13	(h)	Middlesbrough	W	4-0	Royle, Marsh 2, Tueart	30,353
8		20	(a)	Derby Co	L	0-1		23,250
9		24	(h)	Stoke C	W	1-0	Marsh	28,915
10		27	(h)	Manchester U	D	2-2	Nicholl (og), Royle	46,931
11	Oct	4	(a)	Arsenal	W	3-2	Hartford, Royle, Marsh	24,928
12		11	(h)	Burnley	D	0-0		35,003
13		18	(a)	Tottenham H	D	2-2	Watson, Bell	30,502
14		25	(h)	Ipswich T	D	1-1	Bell	30,644
15	Nov	1	(a)	Sheffield U	D	2-2	Booth, Barnes	24,670
16		8	(h)	Birmingham C	W	2-0	Bell 2	28,329
17		15	(a)	Everton	D	1-1	Booth	32,077
18		22	(h)	Tottenham H	W	2-1	Tueart, Oakes	31,456
19		29	(a)	Wolverhampton W	W	4-0	Hartford 2, Barnes, Tueart	20,867
20	Dec	6	(h)	Q.P.R.	D	0-0		36,066
21		13	(h)	Coventry C	W	4-2	Oakes, Barnes, Booth, Tueart	27,256
22		20	(a)	Norwich C	D	2-2	Tueart, Royle	19,692
23		26	(h)	Leeds U	L	0-1		48,077
24		27	(a)	Liverpool	L	0-1		53,386
25	Jan	10	(a)	Middlesbrough	L	0-1		23,000
26		17	(h)	West Ham U	W	3-0	Royle 2 (1 pen), Oakes	32,147
27		31	(a)	Leicester C	L	0-1		21,723
28	Feb	7	(h)	Aston Villa	W	2-1	Booth, Hartford	32,331
29		14	(a)	Birmingham C	L	1-2	Hartford	22,445
30		21	(h)	Everton	W	3-0	Hartford, Tueart (pen), Royle	33,148
31	Mar	6	(h)	Sheffield U	W	4-0	Hartford 2, Tueart, Royle	33,510
32		13	(a)	Burnley	D	0-0		24,278
33		20	(h)	Wolverhampton W	W	3-2	Keegan, Tueart (pen), Doyle	32,761
34		27	(a)	Q.P.R.	L	0-1		29,883
35	Apr	2	(a)	Stoke C	D	0-0		18,798
36		7	(a)	Ipswich T	L	1-2	Keegan	21,290
37		10	(h)	Derby Co	W	4-3	Tueart 2, Royle, Power	42,061
38		14	(a)	Newcastle U	L	1-2	Royle	21,095
39		17	(a)	Leeds U	L	1-2	Bell	33,514
40		19	(h)	Liverpool	L	0-3		50,439
41		24	(h)	Arsenal	W	3-1	Booth 2, Hartford	31,003
42	May	4	(a)	Manchester U	L	0-2		59,528

FINAL LEAGUE POSITION: 8th in Division One

Appearances

Sub. Appearances

Goals

Corrigan	Hammond	Donachie	Doyle	Watson	Oakes	Hartford	Bell	Marsh	Royle	Tueart	Telford	Clements	Power	Leman	Barnes	Booth	MacRae	Keegan	Barrett	Owen	Docherty	
1	2	3	4	5	6	7	8	9	10	11												1
1	2	3	4	5	6	7	8	9	10	11												2
1	2	3	4	5	6	7	8	9	10*	11	12											3
1		3	4	5	6	7	8	9		11		2	10									4
1		3	4	5	6	7	8	9	10	11		2										5
1		3	4	5	6	7	8	10		11		2		9								6
1		3	4	5	6	7	8	10	9	11		2										7
1		3	4	5	6	7	8	10	9	11		2										8
1		3	4	5	6	7	8	10	9	11		2										9
1		3	4	5	6	7	8	10	9*	11		2		12								10
1		3	4	5	6	7	8	10	9	11*		2	12									11
1		3	4	5	6	7	8	9	10*			2		12	11							12
1		3	4	9	6	10	8			11		2			7	5						13
1		3	4	9	6	7	8			11		2			10	5						14
		3	4	5	6	10	8			11		2			7	9	1					15
1		3	4	5	6	7	8		10	9		2			11							16
1		3	4	5	6	7			10	11*		2	12		8	9						17
1		3	4	5	6	10			9	11		2	8		7							18
1		3	4	5	6	10			9	11		2	8		7							19
1		3	4	5	6	10			9	11		2			7	8						20
1	2	3	4	5	6	10			9	11			12		7	8*						21
1		3	4	5	6	10			9	11		2			7	8						22
1		3	4	5	6	10			9	11		2	12		7*	8						23
1		3	4	5	6*	10			9	11		2	7			8		12				24
1		3	4	5	6	10			9				7			8		11	2			25
1		3	4		6	10			9			5	7		11			8	2			26
1		3	4	5	6*	10			9	11			7		12	8			2			27
1		3	4	5	6	10			9	11		2*			8	12		7				28
1		3	4	5	6	10			9			2			11	8		7				29
1		3	4	5	6	10			9	11					7	8		2				30
1		3	4	5	6	10			9	11					7	8		2				31
1		3	4	5	6	10			9	11					7	8		2				32
1		3	4			10			9	11		5			7	8		2		6		33
1		3	4		6	10			9*	11		12			7	5		2		8		34
1	2	3	4		6				9	11			10		7	5		8				35
1	2	3	4			6			9	11			6		7	5		8				36
1	12	3	4		6		2		9	11			10		7*	5		8				37
1	2				3				9	11		4	10		7	5		8		6		38
1		2	4		3	10	8		9	11			7			5		6				39
1		2	4		3*	10	8		9	11			12		7	5		6				40
1		3	4			10	8		9	12			6*		7	5		2		11		41
1			4*		12	10			9	11		2	8		7	5		6			3	42
41	7	40	41	31	38	39	20	12	37	37		26	14	1	27	25	1	17	3	4	1	
	1				1					1	1	1	5	2	1	1		1				
			1	1	3	9	6	4	12	14			1		3	6		2				

1976-77

1	Aug	21	(a)	Leicester C	D	2-2	Tueart, Royle	22,612
2		25	(h)	Aston Villa	W	2-0	Tueart, Watson	41,007
3		28	(h)	Stoke C	D	0-0		39,878
4	Sep	4	(a)	Arsenal	D	0-0		35,132
5		11	(h)	Bristol C	W	2-1	Tueart, Barnes	35,891
6		18	(a)	Sunderland	W	2-0	Tueart, Royle	37,395
7		25	(h)	Manchester U	L	1-3	Tueart	48,861
8	Oct	2	(h)	West Ham U	W	4-2	Owen, Tueart 2, Hartford	37,795
9		5	(a)	Everton	D	2-2	Hartford, Power	31,370
10		16	(h)	Q.P.R.	D	0-0		40,751
11		23	(a)	Ipswich T	L	0-1		25,041
12		30	(a)	Norwich C	W	2-0	Kidd, Royle	22,861
13	Nov	6	(h)	Newcastle U	D	0-0		40,049
14		20	(h)	W.B.A.	W	1-0	Tueart	36,656
15		27	(a)	Birmingham C	D	0-0		29,722
16	Dec	4	(h)	Derby Co	W	3-2	Kidd 2, Tueart	34,179
17		7	(a)	Middlesbrough	D	0-0		18,000
18		11	(a)	Tottenham H	D	2-2	Kidd, Power	24,608
19		18	(h)	Coventry C	W	2-0	Kidd, Tueart	32,527
20		27	(a)	Leeds U	W	2-0	Kidd 2	48,708
21		29	(h)	Liverpool	D	1-1	Royle	50,020
22	Jan	22	(h)	Leicester C	W	5-0	Kidd 4, Doyle	37,609
23	Feb	5	(a)	Stoke C	W	2-0	Tueart, Royle	27,139
24		12	(h)	Arsenal	W	1-0	Royle	45,368
25		16	(a)	Newcastle U	D	2-2	Tueart, Kidd	27,920
26		19	(a)	Bristol C	L	0-1		27,601
27	Mar	1	(h)	Norwich C	W	2-0	Tueart 2 (2 pens)	36,021
28		5	(a)	Manchester U	L	1-3	Royle	58,595
29		9	(h)	Sunderland	W	1-0	Tueart (pen)	44,439
30		12	(a)	West Ham U	L	0-1		24,974
31		22	(a)	Q.P.R.	D	0-0		17,619
32	Apr	2	(h)	Ipswich T	W	2-1	Kidd, Watson	42,780
33		8	(h)	Leeds U	W	2-1	Kidd 2	47,727
34		9	(a)	Liverpool	L	1-2	Kidd	55,283
35		11	(h)	Middlesbrough	W	1-0	Hartford	37,735
36		16	(a)	W.B.A.	W	2-0	Tueart, Kidd	24,889
37		19	(h)	Birmingham C	W	2-1	Kidd 2	36,203
38		30	(a)	Derby Co	L	0-4		29,127
39	May	4	(a)	Aston Villa	D	1-1	Tueart	36,190
40		7	(h)	Tottenham H	W	5-0	Booth, Tueart, Barnes, Hartford, Kidd	37,919
41		10	(h)	Everton	D	1-1	Kidd	38,440
42		14	(a)	Coventry C	W	1-0	Conway	21,429

FINAL LEAGUE POSITION: 2nd in Division One

Appearances

Sub. Appearances

Goals

Corrigan	Docherty	Donachie	Doyle	Watson	Power	Conway	Kidd	Royle	Hartford	Tueart	Barnes	Booth	Henry	Keegan	Clements	Owen	Lester	
1	2	3	4	5	6	7	8	9	10	11								1
1	2	3	4	5	6	7	9	10	8	11								2
1	2	3	4	5	6	7		10	8	11	9							3
1	2	3	4	5	6	7		9	10	11		8						4
1	2	3	4	5		6	8	9	10	11	7							5
1	2	3	4	5	6	7*	8	9	10	11			12					6
1	2	3	4	5	6		8	9	10	11		12		7*				7
1		3	4	5			8	9	10	11	7				2	6		8
1		3	4	5	7		8	9	10	11					2	6		9
1		3	4	5	7		8	9*	10	11					2	6	12	10
1		3	4	5	6		8	9	10	11					2	7		11
1		3	4	5	6		8	9	10	11					2	7		12
1		3	4	5	6*		10	9	8	11	12				2	7		13
1		3	4	5	12	6	8	9*	10	11					2	7		14
1		3	4	5	7		8	9	10	11					2	6		15
1		3	4	5	7		8	9	10	11	12				2*	6		16
1		3	4	5	6	7	8	9	10	11					2			17
1		3	4	5	6		8	9	10	11					2	7		18
1		3	4	5	6		8	9	10	11					2	7		19
1		3	4	5	6		8	9	10	11					2	7		20
1		3	4	5	6		8	9	10	11					2	7		21
1		3	4	5	6		8	9	10	11*	12				2	7		22
1		3	4	5	6		8	9	10	11					2	7		23
1		3	4	5	6		8	9	10	11					2	7		24
1		3	4	5	6		8	9	10	11					2	7		25
1		3	4	5	6		8	9	10	11					2	7		26
1		3	4	5	6		8	9	10	11					2	7		27
1		3	4	5	6*		8	9	10	11	12				2	7		28
1		3	4				8	9	10	11	7	5			2	6		29
1		3	4*	5		6	8	9	10	11	7				2	12		30
1		3		5		6	8	9	10	11	7	4			2			31
1		3		5			8	9	10		7	4	12	6	2	11*		32
1		3	4	5			8	9	10	11	7	6			2			33
1		3	4	5	11		8	9*	10		12	6		7	2			34
1		3		5			8		10	11	7	4		8	2	6		35
1		3		5			8		10	11	7	4		8	2	6		36
1		3		5			8		10	11	7	4		8	2	6		37
1		3	6	5	12		8	9*			7	4		11	2	10		38
1		3		5		12	8*	9		11	7	4		10	2	6		39
1		3		5		12	8	9*	10	11	7	4			2	6		40
1		3		5			8	9	10	11	7	4			2	6		41
1		3		5	8	7		9	10		11	4		8	2	6		42
42	7	42	33	41	27	11	39	39	40	38	16	14		8	35	30		
					2	2					5	1	2			1	1	
			1	2	2	1	21	7	4	18	2	1				1		

1977-78

1	Aug	20	(h)	Leicester C	D	0-0		45,993
2		24	(a)	Aston Villa	W	4-1	Booth, Tueart 3	40,121
3		27	(a)	West Ham U	W	1-0	Royle	25,278
4	Sep	3	(h)	Norwich C	W	4-0	Channon 2, Power, Hartford	41,269
5		10	(h)	Manchester U	W	3-1	Kidd 2, Channon	50,856
6		17	(a)	Q.P.R.	D	1-1	Royle	24,668
7		24	(h)	Bristol C	W	2-0	Barnes, Owen	41,897
8	Oct	1	(a)	Everton	D	1-1	Hartford	43,285
9		4	(a)	Coventry C	L	2-4	Tueart, Barnes	19,586
10		8	(h)	Arsenal	W	2-1	Barnes, Tueart (pen)	43,177
11		15	(a)	Nottingham F	L	1-2	Kidd	35,572
12		22	(h)	Wolverhampton W	L	0-2		42,730
13		29	(h)	Liverpool	W	3-1	Kidd, Channon, Royle	49,207
14	Nov	5	(a)	Ipswich T	L	0-1		23,636
15		12	(h)	Leeds U	L	2-3	Channon, Barnes	42,651
16		19	(a)	W.B.A.	D	0-0		27,159
17		26	(h)	Chelsea	W	6-2	Wilkins G (og), Tueart 3, Channon, Barnes	34,354
18	Dec	3	(a)	Derby Co	L	1-2	Power	26,888
19		10	(h)	Birmingham C	W	3-0	Tueart, Owen, Channon	36,671
20		17	(a)	Leeds U	L	0-2		37,380
21		26	(h)	Newcastle U	W	4-0	Tueart 3, Kidd	45,811
22		27	(a)	Middlesbrough	W	2-0	Hartford, Owen	26,879
23		31	(h)	Aston Villa	W	2-0	Barnes, Kidd	46,074
24	Jan	2	(a)	Leicester C	W	1-0	Owen (pen)	24,041
25		14	(h)	West Ham U	W	3-2	Kidd, Booth, Barnes	43,627
26		21	(a)	Norwich C	W	3-1	Kidd 2, Owen	20,397
27	Feb	11	(h)	Q.P.R.	W	2-1	Channon, Bell	39,860
28		17	(a)	Bristol C	D	2-2	Kidd, Booth	25,834
29		25	(h)	Everton	W	1-0	Kidd	46,817
30	Mar	4	(a)	Arsenal	L	0-3		34,003
31		15	(a)	Manchester U	D	2-2	Barnes, Kidd	58,426
32		18	(a)	Wolverhampton W	D	1-1	Bell	20,583
33		25	(h)	Middlesbrough	D	2-2	Channon 2	37,944
34		29	(a)	Newcastle U	D	2-2	Palmer 2	20,246
35	Apr	1	(h)	Ipswich T	W	2-1	Palmer, Channon	34,975
36		11	(h)	Nottingham F	D	0-0		43,428
37		15	(h)	W.B.A.	L	1-3	Kidd	36,521
38		22	(a)	Birmingham C	W	4-1	Owen (pen), Kidd 2, Power	25,294
39		25	(h)	Coventry C	W	3-1	Kidd, Hartford, Owen (pen)	32,412
40		29	(h)	Derby Co	D	1-1	Channon	39,175
41	May	1	(a)	Liverpool	L	0-4		44,528
42		5	(a)	Chelsea	D	0-0		18,782

FINAL LEAGUE POSITION: 4th in Division One

Appearances

Sub. Appearances

Goals

Corrigan	Clements	Donachie	Doyle	Watson	Booth	Owen	Channon	Royle	Hartford	Tueart	Kidd	Barnes	Power	Henry	Keegan	Bell	Palmer	
1	2	3	4	5	6	7	8	9	10	11								1
1	2	3	4	5	6		8	9	10	11	7							2
1	2	3	4	5	6		8	9	10	11	7							3
1	2	3		5	6	4	8		10		9	7	11					4
1	2	3		5	6	4	8		10		9	7	11					5
1	2	3		5	6	4	8	9	10		7	11						6
1	2		3	5	6	4	8		10		9	7	11					7
1	2	3		5	6*	4		12	10	11	9	7	8					8
1	2	3		5	6			9	10	11	4	7	8					9
1	2	3		5	6	4			10	11	9	7	8					10
1	12	3	5		6	4	8		10	11*	9	7	2					11
1	12	3	2	5	6	4	8				9	7	11	10*				12
1	2	3	6	5		4	8	9			10	7	11					13
1	2	3	4	5		6	8		10		9	7	11					14
1	2	3	4	5			8		10	11	9	7	6					15
1	2	3		5	4		8		10	11	9	7	6					16
1	2	3		5	4		8		10	11	9	7	6					17
1	2	3		5	4		8		10	11	9	7	6					18
1	2	3		5	4	7	8		10	11	9		6					19
1	2	3		5	4	7	8		10*	11	9		6		12			20
1	2	3		5	4	8			10	11	9	7	6*			12		21
1	2	3		5	4	6			10		9	7				8	11	22
1	2	3		5	4	6			10	11	9	7				8		23
1	2	3	12	5	4	6			10		9	7*				8	11	24
1	2*	3		5	4	6	12		10	11	9	7				8		25
1	2	3		5	4	6			10	11	9	7				8		26
1	2	3		5	4	6	7		10		9	11				8		27
1	2	3		5	4	6	7		10		9	11				8		28
1	2	3		5	4		7		10		9	11	6			8		29
1	2	3		5	4		7		10		9	11	6			8		30
1	2	3		5	4	6	7		10		9	11				8		31
1	2	3		5	4	6	7				9	11	10			8		32
1	2	3		5	4	6	7				9*	11	10		12	8		33
1	2	3	4	5	8	6	7					11	10				9	34
1	2	3	4	5	8	6	7		10			11					9	35
1	2		4	5	8	6	7		10		9	11	3					36
1	2		4	5	8*	6	7		10		9	11	3				12	37
1	2	3		5	4	6	7		10		9		11			8		38
1	2	3		5	4	6	7		10		9		11			8		39
1	2	3		5	4	6*	7		10		9	12	11			8		40
1	2	3		5	4	6	7		10		9		11			8		41
1	2	3		5	4	6	8		10		9	7	11					42
42	40	39	13	41	39	33	33	6	37	17	39	33	29	1		16	4	
	2		1				1	1				1			2	1	1	
					3	7	12	3	4	12	16	8	3			2	3	

1978-79

1	Aug	19	(a)	Derby Co	D 1-1	Kidd	26,480
2		22	(h)	Arsenal	D 1-1	Kidd	39,506
3		26	(h)	Liverpool	L 1-4	Kidd	46,710
4	Sep	2	(a)	Norwich C	D 1-1	Channon	18,607
5		9	(h)	Leeds U	W 3-0	Watson, Palmer 2	40,125
6		16	(a)	Chelsea	W 4-1	Channon, Futcher R 3	28,980
7		23	(h)	Tottenham H	W 2-0	Owen, Futcher R	43,471
8		30	(a)	Manchester U	L 0-1		55,317
9	Oct	7	(a)	Birmingham C	W 2-1	Kidd, Futcher R	18,378
10		14	(h)	Coventry C	W 2-0	Owen 2 (2 pens)	36,723
11		21	(a)	Bolton W	D 2-2	Palmer, Owen	32,249
12		28	(h)	W.B.A.	D 2-2	Channon, Hartford	40,521
13	Nov	4	(a)	Aston Villa	D 1-1	Owen (pen)	32,724
14		11	(h)	Derby Co	L 1-2	Owen (pen)	37,376
15		18	(a)	Liverpool	L 0-1		47,765
16		25	(h)	Ipswich T	L 1-2	Hartford	38,256
17	Dec	9	(h)	Southampton	L 1-2	Power	33,450
18		16	(a)	Q.P.R.	L 1-2	Channon	12,902
19		23	(h)	Nottingham F	D 0-0		37,012
20		26	(a)	Everton	L 0-1		46,997
21		30	(a)	Bristol C	D 1-1	Futcher R	25,253
22	Jan	13	(a)	Leeds U	D 1-1	Kidd	36,303
23		20	(h)	Chelsea	L 2-3	Power, Futcher R	31,876
24	Feb	3	(a)	Tottenham H	W 3-0	Kidd (pen), Barnes, Channon	32,037
25		10	(h)	Manchester U	L 0-3		46,151
26		24	(a)	Coventry C	W 3-0	Channon 2, Kidd	20,116
27		27	(h)	Norwich C	D 2-2	Owen 2 (1 pen)	30,012
28	Mar	3	(h)	Bolton W	W 2-1	Channon, Owen (pen)	41,127
29		24	(a)	Arsenal	D 1-1	Channon	35,014
30		27	(a)	Wolverhampton W	D 1-1	Channon	19,998
31		31	(a)	Ipswich T	L 1-2	Silkman	20,773
32	Apr	4	(a)	W.B.A.	L 0-4		22,314
33		7	(h)	Wolverhampton W	W 3-1	Channon, Palmer, Silkman	32,298
34		14	(h)	Everton	D 0-0		39,711
35		17	(a)	Middlesbrough	L 0-2		19,676
36		21	(h)	Q.P.R.	W 3-1	Silkman, Owen 2	30,694
37		24	(h)	Middlesbrough	W 1-0	Deyna	28,264
38		28	(a)	Southampton	L 0-1		19,744
39	May	1	(h)	Birmingham C	W 3-1	Power, Deyna 2	27,366
40		5	(h)	Bristol C	W 2-0	Deyna, Hartford	29,739
41		9	(a)	Nottingham F	L 1-3	Lloyd (og)	21,104
42		15	(h)	Aston Villa	L 2-3	Deyna 2	30,028

FINAL LEAGUE POSITION: 15th in Division One

Appearances

Sub. Appearances

Goals

Corrigan	Clements	Donachie	Keegan	Watson	Futcher P	Channon	Hartford	Kidd	Power	Barnes	Booth	Owen	Futcher R	Palmer	Viljoen	Henry	Bell	Deyna	Ranson	Reid	Silkman	Bennett	
1	2	3	4	5	6	7	8	9	10	11													1
1	2	3	4	5	6	7	10	9	8	11													2
1	2	3	4		6	7	8	9	11		5	10											3
1	2	3			6	7	8		4	11	5	10	9										4
1	2	3		5	6	7	10		4	11		8		9									5
1		2		5	6	7	10		3	11*		8	9		4	12							6
1	2	3		5	6	7	10		11			8	9		4								7
1	2	3		5	6	7	10	9	4	11		8											8
1	2	3		5		7	10	8		11*	4	6	9			12							9
1	2	3		5			10	6		11	4	8	9	7									10
1	2	3		5			8	10		11	6	7	12	9*	4								11
1	2	3			6	7	10	9			5	8	12	11	4*								12
1	2	3			6	7	10	9			5	8		11	4								13
1	2	3		5		7	10	9		11	4	6					8						14
1	2	3		5		7*	10	9		11	4	6	12	8									15
1	2*	3		5			10	9	6	11	4	7		12				8					16
1		3	2	5		7	10	9*	6	11	4	12			8								17
1		3		5	2	7	10		6	11	4	8	12					9*					18
1		3		5	4	7	10		6	11		8	9						2				19
1		3		5	6	7	10*		4	11		8	9	12					2				20
1		3		5	4	7	10		6	11		8	9						2				21
1		3		5*	6	7	10	12	4	11		8	9						2				22
1		2			6	7	10	9	3	11	5*	4	12					8					23
1		2		5*	6	7	10	9	3	11		4					8	12					24
1		2		5	6	7	10	9	3	11		8					4						25
1		2			6	7	10	9	3	11	5	4			8								26
1		2			6	7	10	9	3	11	5	4			8								27
1		2		5		7	10	9	3	11	6	4			8								28
1		2		5		7	10		3		6	4			8	9		11					29
1				5		7	10		3	11		4	9*	12	8	6			2				30
1				5		7	10		3	11		8	12			6*			2	4	9		31
1		2*			6	7	10		3		5			11	8	4				12	9		32
1		3			6	7*	10				5	8	12	11		4				2	9		33
1				5	2		10		3	11	4*			7	8	6					9	12	34
1				5	6		10		3	11				7*	8	4		12	2		9		35
1		2		5			10		3	11		7			4		6	8			9		36
1		3		5		7			11			8				4	6	10		2	9		37
1		3		5		7			11			8				10	6	4		2	9		38
1		3		5		7			11			8				4	6	10		2	9		39
1		3		5		7	10		11							4	6	8		2	9		40
1		3		5		7	10					11				4	6	8		2	9		41
1		3		5*		7	10							12	8	4	6	11	2		9		42
42	15	38	4	33	24	36	39	19	32	29	20	34	10	10	16	13	10	11	8	7	12		
								1				1	7	4		2		2		1		1	
				1		11	3	7	3	1		11	7	4				6			3		

1979-80

1	Aug	18	(h)	Crystal Palace	D	0-0		40,681
2		21	(a)	Middlesbrough	L	0-3		24,002
3		25	(h)	Brighton & H.A.	W	3-2	Power, Channon, Robinson (pen)	34,557
4	Sep	1	(a)	Tottenham H	L	1-2	MacKenzie	30,901
5		8	(h)	Southampton	L	0-1		34,920
6		15	(a)	W.B.A.	L	0-4		22,236
7		22	(h)	Coventry C	W	3-0	Robinson 2, MacKenzie	30,869
8		29	(a)	Leeds U	W	2-1	Power, Deyna	29,592
9	Oct	6	(a)	Arsenal	D	0-0		34,688
10		10	(h)	Middlesbrough	W	1-0	Deyna	29,384
11		13	(h)	Nottingham F	W	1-0	Deyna	41,683
12		20	(a)	Norwich C	D	2-2	Bennett 2	18,000
13		27	(h)	Liverpool	L	0-4		48,128
14	Nov	3	(a)	Crystal Palace	L	0-2		29,443
15		10	(h)	Manchester U	W	2-0	Henry, Robinson	50,067
16		17	(a)	Bolton W	W	1-0	Daley	25,515
17		24	(a)	Bristol C	L	0-1		18,296
18	Dec	1	(h)	Wolverhampton W	L	2-3	Palmer, Deyna	33,984
19		8	(a)	Ipswich T	L	0-4		18,221
20		15	(h)	Derby Co	W	3-0	Robinson, Henry, Webb (og)	27,664
21		22	(a)	Everton	W	2-1	Daley, Henry	26,305
22		26	(h)	Stoke C	D	1-1	Power	36,286
23		29	(a)	Brighton & H.A.	L	1-4	Lee	28,093
24	Jan	12	(h)	Tottenham H	D	1-1	Robinson (pen)	34,837
25		19	(a)	Southampton	L	1-4	Power	21,422
26	Feb	2	(h)	W.B.A.	L	1-3	Lee	32,904
27		9	(a)	Coventry C	D	0-0		17,114
28		16	(h)	Leeds U	D	1-1	Power	34,392
29		23	(a)	Nottingham F	L	0-4		27,255
30		27	(a)	Aston Villa	D	2-2	Robinson (pen), Power	29,139
31	Mar	1	(h)	Norwich C	D	0-0		32,248
32		11	(a)	Liverpool	L	0-2		40,443
33		15	(h)	Arsenal	L	0-3		33,792
34		22	(a)	Manchester U	L	0-1		56,384
35		29	(h)	Bolton W	D	2-2	Tueart 2	33,500
36	Apr	2	(h)	Everton	D	1-1	Deyna	33,437
37		5	(a)	Stoke C	D	0-0		20,451
38		7	(h)	Aston Villa	D	1-1	Power	42,584
39		12	(a)	Wolverhampton W	W	2-1	Reeves, Tueart (pen)	23,850
40		19	(h)	Bristol C	W	3-1	Robinson, Deyna, Tueart	32,745
41		26	(a)	Derby Co	L	1-3	Tueart	22,572
42	May	3	(h)	Ipswich T	W	2-1	Reeves, Henry	31,648
FINAL LEAGUE POSITION: 17th in Division One								Appearances
								Sub. Appearances
								Goals

Corrigan	Ranson	Stepanovic	Caton	Booth	Power	MacKenzie	Silkman	Robinson	Deyna	Henry	Viljoen	Channon	Donachie	Daley	Lee	Futcher	Bennett	Shinton	Reid	Palmer	Tueart	Reeves	Sugrue	
1	2*	3	4	5	6	7	8	9	10	11	12													1
1	2	3	4	5	6	7	8	9	10*	11	12													2
1	2	3	4	5	6	7	8	9			10	11												3
1	2	3	4	5	6	7	8	9		12	10*	11												4
1	2	3	4		6	7	8	9*		12			5	10	11									5
1	2	3	4		6*	7	8	9					5	10	11	12								6
1	2	4	5		10	7		9					3	8		6	11							7
1	2	4	5		10	7		9	11				3	8		6								8
1	2	4*	5		10	7		9	11					8		6	12	3						9
1	2	3	5		10	7		9	11					8		6		4						10
1	2		5		10	7		9	11		8					6	4		3					11
1	2	12	5		3	7*		9	11		8					6	10		4					12
1	2		5		3	7		9	11		8					6	4		10					13
1	2		5		3	7	11	9		12				8		6	4		10*					14
1	2		5	6	10			9	11	7			3	8			4							15
1	2	6	5		10			9	11	7			3	8			4							16
1	2	6	5		10			9	11	7			3	8			4							17
1	2	6*	5	4					10	7			3	8	12		9			11				18
1	2		5	6	3			9		7	10			8			4			11				19
1	2		5	6	11			9		7			3	8			4	10						20
1	2		5	4	10			9		7			3	8			6	11						21
1	2		5	6	10			9		7			3	8			4	11						22
1	2		5	6	9					7			3	8	11		4		10					23
1			5		3	12		9		7*	10		2	8	11		6		4					24
1	2		5	6	7			9			10*		3	8	11				4	12				25
1	2		5	4	10			9		7			3	8	11				6					26
1	2		5	6	10	7		9		4			3	8			11							27
1	2		5	6	10	7				4			3	8*			11		12	9				28
1	2		5	6	10			8		7			3				11		4	9				29
1	2		5	6	10			9		7			3	8			11		4					30
1	2		5	6*	10			8	12	7				3			9		4		11			31
1	2		5		3				9	7	6			8			11		4		10			32
1	2		5	4	6			12	8	7							9		3		11*	10		33
1	2		5	4	6					7				8			11*		3	12	10	9		34
1	2		5	4	6					7				8					3	11	10	9		35
1	2		5	4	6				9	7				8					3		10	11		36
1	2		5	4	6				9	7				8					3		10	11		37
1	2		5	4	6				9	7				8					3		10	11		38
1	2		5		6				9	7				8		4			3		10	11		39
1	2		5		6			11	9	7				8		4			3		10			40
1	2		5		6	12			9*	7				8		4			3		10	11		41
1			5		3	7			9	6*				8		4	12		2			11	10	42
42	20	13	42	24	41	17	7	29	21	29	9	2	19	33	6	12	23	5	22	5	11	9	1	
		1				2		1	1	3	2				1	1	2		1	2				
					7	2		8	6	4		1		2	2		2			1	5	2		

1980-81

1	Aug	16	(a)	Southampton	L 0-3		23,320
2		20	(h)	Sunderland	L 0-4		33,271
3		23	(h)	Aston Villa	D 2-2	Tueart (pen), Ranson	30,017
4		30	(a)	Middlesbrough	D 2-2	Reeves, MacKenzie	15,761
5	Sep	6	(h)	Arsenal	D 1-1	Tueart (pen)	32,233
6		13	(a)	Nottingham F	L 2-3	Bennett, Henry	23,184
7		20	(h)	Stoke C	L 1-2	Tueart	29,507
8		27	(a)	Manchester U	D 2-2	Reeves, Palmer	55,926
9	Oct	4	(h)	Liverpool	L 0-3		41,022
10		8	(a)	Leeds U	L 0-1		19,134
11		11	(a)	W.B.A.	L 1-3	Daley	19,515
12		18	(h)	Birmingham C	L 0-1		30,041
13		22	(h)	Tottenham H	W 3-1	Reeves, Daley, MacKenzie	28,788
14		25	(a)	Brighton & H.A.	W 2-1	Tueart 2	18,368
15	Nov	1	(h)	Norwich C	W 1-0	Power	33,056
16		8	(a)	Leicester C	D 1-1	Tueart	19,104
17		12	(a)	Sunderland	L 0-2		23,387
18		15	(h)	Southampton	W 3-0	Gow, Bennett, Reeves	32,661
19		22	(h)	Coventry C	W 3-0	Reeves, Power, Bennett	30,047
20		29	(a)	Crystal Palace	W 3-2	Reeves, Gow 2	16,575
21	Dec	6	(h)	Ipswich T	D 1-1	Gow	35,215
22		13	(a)	Tottenham H	L 1-2	Boyer	23,883
23		20	(h)	Leeds U	W 1-0	Reeves	31,866
24		26	(a)	Everton	W 2-0	Gow, Power	36,194
25		27	(h)	Wolverhampton W	W 4-0	McDonald, Hutchison 2, Reeves	37,817
26	Jan	10	(a)	Coventry C	D 1-1	MacKenzie	18,248
27		17	(h)	Middlesbrough	W 3-2	Reeves, Hutchison, McDonald	30,774
28		31	(a)	Aston Villa	L 0-1		33,682
29	Feb	7	(h)	Nottingham Forest	D 1-1	Power	39,524
30		21	(h)	Manchester U	W 1-0	MacKenzie	50,114
31		24	(a)	Arsenal	L 0-2		24,790
32	Mar	14	(h)	W.B.A.	W 2-1	McDonald, Tueart	36,581
33		18	(a)	Stoke C	L 1-2	McDonald	15,842
34		21	(a)	Birmingham C	L 0-2		16,160
35		28	(h)	Brighton & H.A.	D 1-1	MacKenzie	30,122
36		31	(h)	Leicester C	D 3-3	Reeves 2, Henry	26,141
37	Apr	4	(a)	Norwich C	L 0-2		17,957
38		18	(a)	Wolverhampton W	W 3-1	Tueart, Bennett 2	17,371
39		20	(h)	Everton	W 3-1	Bennett, Reeves, MacKenzie	34,434
40		25	(a)	Ipswich T	L 0-1		22,684
41	May	2	(h)	Crystal Palace	D 1-1	Bennett	31,017
42		19	(a)	Liverpool	L 0-1		24,462

FINAL LEAGUE POSITION: 12th in Division One

Appearances

Sub. Appearances

Goals

Corrigan	Ranson	Caton	Reid	Booth	Henry	Tueart	Daley	Sugrue	Power	Reeves	Stepanovic	MacKenzie	Palmer	MacRae	Bennett	Deyna	Buckley	McDonald	Hutchison	Gow	Boyer	Williams	Kinsey	May	
1	2	3	4	5	6	7	8	9	10	11															1
1		3	2	5	6	7	8	9	10	11	4														2
1	2	5	3	4		7	8	9*	10	11		6	12												3
	2	5	3	4	6		8		10	11		9		1	7										4
		5	2	4	6	7	8		3	11		9		1	10										5
		5	2	4	6	7	8		3	11		9		1	10										6
1		5	2	4	6*	7	8		3			9	12		10	11									7
1	2	5	3	4	6		8	12	7	11			9		10*										8
1	2	5	3	4	6		8		7	11		9	10												9
1	2	5	3	4	6		8		7	11		9	10*			12									10
1	2	5	3	4	6		8		7	11		9				10									11
1	2	5	4	6	7		8		3	11		9			10										12
1	12	6	2	5*	4	7	8		3	11		9					10								13
1	2	6	4			7	8		5	11		9						3	10						14
1	2	5	4			7	12		6			8			11			3	10*	9					15
1	2	5*	4			9			11	10		6			12			3	7	8					16
1	2		4	6		7*			5	11		9			12			3	10	8					17
1	2		4	6					5	11		9			7			3	10	8					18
1	2		4	6	12				5	11		9			7*			3	10	8					19
1	2		4	6					5	11		9			7			3	10	8					20
1	2		4	6		10*			5	11		9						3	7	8	12				21
1	2		4	6					5	11		9*			12			3	10	8	7				22
1	2		4	6*	12				5	11		9						3	10	8	7				23
1	2	6	4						5	11		9						3	10	8	7				24
1	2	6	4						5	11		9						3	10	8	7				25
1	2	6	4						5	11		9						3	10	8	7				26
1	2*	6	4						5	11		9			12			3	10	8	7				27
1		5		4	2				3	11		9			7			3	10	8					28
1		6		4	2	7			5	11		9						3	10	8					29
1			4	6	2				5	11		9			7			3	10	8					30
1	2	6	4			12			5	11		9			7			3*	10	8					31
	2	6	4		10	7			5	11		9					12	3		8*		1			32
1	2	12	4	6	10	7			5	11		9*					8	3							33
1	2*	6		4	8	7			5	11		9			12			3	10						34
1	2	6	4		8	7*			5	11		9			12			3	10						35
1	2	6	4		8				5	11		9			7			3	10						36
1	2		4	6	8				5	11		9			7			3	10						37
1		6*		4	2	8			5	11		9			7		12	3					10		38
1			4	6	2	8		11*	5	12		9			7		10	3							39
1	2		4	6	3	8			5	11		9			7		10*							12	40
1	2	6			4				5	11		9			7			3	10	8					41
	2		4	6		11			5			9			7			3	10	8		1			42
37	32	29	37	30	25	21	14	4	42	38	1	39	3	3	20	2	4	28	24	20	6	2	1		
	1	1			2	1	1	1		1			2		6	1	2				1			1	
	1				2	8	2		4	12		6	1		7			4	3	5	1				

1981-82

No.	Month	Day	Venue	Opponents	Result	Scorers	Attendance
1	Aug	29	(h)	W.B.A.	W 2-1	Hutchison, Tueart	36,187
2	Sep	1	(a)	Notts Co	D 1-1	McDonald	14,546
3		5	(a)	Stoke C	W 3-1	Francis 2, Boyer	25,256
4		12	(h)	Southampton	D 1-1	Reeves	42,003
5		19	(a)	Birmingham C	L 0-3		20,109
6		23	(h)	Leeds U	W 4-0	Tueart 2, Reeves 2	35,077
7		26	(h)	Tottenham H	L 0-1		39,085
8	Oct	3	(a)	Brighton & H.A.	L 1-4	Reeves	18,300
9		10	(h)	Manchester U	D 0-0		52,037
10		17	(a)	Arsenal	L 0-1		25,470
11		24	(h)	Nottingham F	D 0-0		34,881
12		31	(a)	Everton	W 1-0	Tueart	31,305
13	Nov	7	(h)	Middlesbrough	W 3-2	Francis, Reeves, Tueart (pen)	32,025
14		21	(h)	Swansea C	W 4-0	Tueart 2 (1 pen), Reeves 2	34,744
15		28	(a)	Ipswich T	L 0-2		20,476
16	Dec	5	(h)	Aston Villa	W 1-0	Tueart	32,487
17		12	(a)	Coventry C	W 1-0	Tueart	12,393
18		19	(h)	Sunderland	L 2-3	Francis 2	29,462
19		26	(a)	Liverpool	W 3-1	Hartford, Bond (pen), Reeves	37,929
20		28	(h)	Wolverhampton W	W 2-1	Hartford, Francis	40,298
21	Jan	9	(h)	Stoke C	D 1-1	Francis	31,941
22		30	(h)	Birmingham C	W 4-2	Francis 2, Reeves 2	28,438
23	Feb	2	(a)	West Ham U	D 1-1	Bond (pen)	26,552
24		6	(a)	Southampton	L 1-2	McDonald	22,645
25		13	(h)	Brighton & H.A.	W 4-0	Francis, Reeves, McDonald, Stevens (og)	30,038
26		20	(a)	Tottenham H	L 0-2		46,181
27		27	(a)	Manchester U	D 1-1	Reeves	57,827
28	Mar	6	(h)	Arsenal	D 0-0		30,288
29		10	(a)	Leeds U	W 1-0	Reeves	20,797
30		13	(a)	Nottingham F	D 1-1	Caton	20,927
31		20	(h)	Everton	D 1-1	Bond	33,002
32		27	(a)	Middlesbrough	D 0-0		11,709
33	Apr	3	(h)	West Ham U	L 0-1		30,875
34		10	(h)	Liverpool	L 0-5		40,112
35		12	(a)	Wolverhampton W	L 1-4	McDonald	14,891
36		17	(a)	Swansea C	L 0-2		19,212
37		21	(a)	W.B.A.	W 1-0	Francis	11,073
38		24	(h)	Ipswich T	D 1-1	Hartford	30,329
39	May	1	(a)	Aston Villa	D 0-0		22,150
40		5	(h)	Notts Co	W 1-0	Power	24,443
41		8	(h)	Coventry C	L 1-3	Francis	27,580
42		15	(a)	Sunderland	L 0-1		26,167

FINAL LEAGUE POSITION: 10th in Division One

Appearances

Sub. Appearances

Goals

Corrigan	Ranson	McDonald	Reid	Power	Caton	O'Neill	Boyer	Tueart	Hutchison	Reeves	Henry	Williams	Gow	Francis	Bond	Booth	Hartford	Hareide	Kinsey	Wilson	Ryan	Jackson	May	Elliott	
1	2	3	4	5	6*	7	8	9	10	11	12														1
	2	3	4	5	6	7	9		10	11*	12	1	8												2
1	2	3	4	5*	6	7	12		10	11			8	9											3
1	2	3	4		6	7	5		10	11			8	9											4
1			4		3	7	12	6	10	11*			8	9	2	5									5
1	2	3	4	5	6	12		7	10	11			8	9*											6
1	2	3	4		6	5	9*	7	10	11			8		12										7
1	2	3	4		6	8	9	7	10	11					5										8
1	2		4	9	5	7		10	6	11					3		8								9
1	2		4	5	6	8		7	9	11					3		10								10
1	2		4	5	6	8*		7	9	11					3		10	12							11
1	2	3	4*	10	6		9	7	12	11					5			8							12
1	2	3	4	8*	6			7	12	11				9	5		10								13
1	2	3	4		6*			7	11	8				9	5		10	12							14
1	2	3	4			6		7	11	8				9	5		10								15
1	2	3	4		6			7	11	8				9	5		10								16
1	2	3	4		6			7	11	8				9	5		10								17
1	2	3	4		6			7*	11	8				9	5		10	12							18
1	2	3	4		6				11	8				9	5		10		7						19
1	2		4		6				11	8				9	5		10		7	3					20
1		3	4		6	7			11	8				9	5		10				2				21
1	2	3		11	6					8				9	5		10		7		4				22
1	2	3		11	6					8				9	5		10	12	7		4*				23
1	2	3		11	6				10*	8				9	5			12	7		4				24
1	2	3	4	11	6					8				9	5*		10		12		7				25
1	2	3	4	11	6					8				9	5*		10				7	12			26
1	2	3	4	11	6					8							10	5			7	9			27
1	2	3	4	11	6					8				9*			10	5			7	12			28
1	2	3	4	11	6					8					5			9			7	10			29
1	2	3	4	11*	6					8					5		10	9	12		7				30
1	2	3	4		6					8				9	5		10	11			7				31
1	2		4		6					8				9				11	7	3		5*	12	10	32
1	2	3	4	5	6					8							10	9			7	11			33
1	2	3	4		6					8					5		10		9	11	7				34
1	2	3								8				9	5		10	4	11		7	6*	12		35
	2	3	4		6					8		1		9	5		10	12	11				7*		36
1	2	3	4	6						8				9	5		10	12	11*		7				37
1	2*	3		4	6					8				9	5		10		11		7		12		38
1		3	4	11	6		9			8					5		10		12		7		2*		39
1		3	4	11	6		9			8					5		10		7		2				40
		3	4	11	6		7			8		1		9	5		10						2		41
1		3		5	6		9			8					4		10		7*	12	2				42
39	36	36	36	25	39	12	10	15	20	42		3	6	26	32	1	30	9	13	3	19	6	3	1	
						1	2		2		2				1			7	3	1		2	3		
		4		1	1		1	9	1	13				12	3		3								

1982-83

1	Aug	28	(a)	Norwich C	W	2-1	Cross, Power	22,638
2	Sep	1	(h)	Stoke C	W	1-0	Cross	27,847
3		4	(h)	Watford	W	1-0	Tueart	29,617
4		7	(a)	Notts Co	L	0-1		9,376
5		11	(a)	Tottenham H	W	2-1	Baker 2	32,483
6		18	(h)	Aston Villa	L	0-1		28,650
7		25	(a)	West Ham U	L	1-4	Boyer	23,883
8	Oct	2	(h)	Coventry C	W	3-2	Baker, Caton, Cross	25,105
9		9	(a)	Everton	L	1-2	Cross	25,158
10		16	(h)	Sunderland	D	2-2	Reeves, Cross	25,053
11		23	(a)	Manchester U	D	2-2	Tueart, Cross	57,334
12		30	(h)	Swansea C	W	2-1	Tueart, Hartford	25,021
13	Nov	6	(h)	Southampton	W	2-0	Reeves, McDonald	25,115
14		13	(a)	Ipswich T	L	0-1		19,523
15		20	(h)	Birmingham C	D	0-0		23,174
16		27	(a)	Nottingham F	L	0-3		18,184
17	Dec	4	(h)	Arsenal	W	2-1	Caton 2	23,057
18		11	(a)	Luton T	L	1-3	Cross	11,013
19		18	(h)	Brighton & H.A.	D	1-1	Bond	20,615
20		27	(a)	Liverpool	L	2-5	Cross, Caton	44,664
21		28	(h)	W.B.A.	W	2-1	Kinsey, Robertson (og)	25,172
22	Jan	1	(a)	Birmingham C	D	2-2	Bond, Bodak	16,362
23		3	(a)	Watford	L	0-2		20,049
24		15	(h)	Norwich C	W	4-1	Cross 2, Bond, Hartford	22,000
25		22	(a)	Aston Villa	D	1-1	Hartford	20,415
26	Feb	5	(h)	Tottenham H	D	2-2	Tueart (pen), Cross	26,357
27		12	(a)	Coventry C	L	0-4		9,527
28		19	(h)	Notts Co	L	0-1		21,199
29		26	(a)	Sunderland	L	2-3	Caton, Reeves	15,144
30	Mar	2	(h)	Everton	D	0-0		22,253
31		5	(h)	Manchester U	L	1-2	Reeves	45,400
32		12	(a)	Swansea C	L	1-4	McDonald	9,884
33		19	(a)	Southampton	L	1-4	Reeves	17,201
34		26	(h)	Ipswich T	L	0-1		21,845
35	Apr	2	(a)	W.B.A.	W	2-0	Cross, Reeves	13,654
36		4	(h)	Liverpool	L	0-4		35,647
37		9	(a)	Stoke C	L	0-1		15,372
38		16	(h)	West Ham U	W	2-0	McDonald, Tueart (pen)	23,015
39		23	(a)	Arsenal	L	0-3		16,810
40		30	(h)	Nottingham F	L	1-2	Baker	23,563
41	May	7	(a)	Brighton & H.A.	W	1-0	Reeves	17,794
42		14	(h)	Luton T	L	0-1		42,843

FINAL LEAGUE POSITION: 20th in Division One

Appearances
Sub. Appearances
Goals

Corrigan	Ranson	McDonald	Baker	Bond	Caton	Hareide	Reeves	Cross	Hartford	Power	Tueart	Williams	Jones	Boyer	Simpson	Reid	Davies	Kinsey	May	Bodak	Park	Golac	Hildersley	Lomax	
1	2	3	4	5	6	7	8	9	10	11															1
1	2	3	4	5	6	7	8	9	10	11															2
1*	2	3	4	5	6	7	8	9	10	11	12														3
	2	3	4	5	6	7	8	9*	10	11	12	1													4
	2	6	7	4	5	3	9		8	11	12	1	10*												5
	2	3*	4	5	6	7	8		10	11	12	1	9												6
	2	3*	4	5	6	7	8		10	11	12	1		9											7
	2		4	6	5		8	9	10	3	7	1			11										8
	2		4		6	10	8	9		3	7	1	11*		12	5									9
1	2				6		8	9	10	5	7				12	4	3	11*							10
1	2	3	11	4	6		8	9	10	5	7														11
1	2	3	11	4	6		8	9	10	5	7														12
1	2	3	11	4	6		8	9	10	5	7														13
1	2	3	11*	4	6		8	9	10	5	7					12									14
1	2	3	11	4	6		8	9	10	5	7														15
1	2	3		10	6		8	9		5	7					4			11						16
1	2	3	11	4	6		8	9	10	5	7														17
1	2	3		11	6		8	9	10	5	7					4									18
1	2	3		4	6		8	9*	10	5	7								12	11					19
1	2	3		4	6		8	9	10	5	7									11					20
1	2	3		6			8	9	10		7					4		5		11					21
1	2	3		6			8	9	10		7					4		5		11					22
1	2	3		6			8		10	5	7					4		9		11					23
1	2			3			8	9	10	5	7					4		6		11					24
1	2			3	6		8	9	10	5	7					4		11							25
1	2	3		5	6		8	9	10		7					4				11					26
	2	3*		5	6		8	9	10			1				4			7	11	12				27
1	2			5	6		8	9	10		7						4		3	11	12				28
1	2	3	9	4	6		8		10		7								5	11					29
1	2	3	9	4	6		8		10		7					4				11					30
1	2	3	11*	5	6		8	9	10		7					4				12					31
1		3	11	5	6		8	9			7					4			12			2	10*		32
			11	5	6		8	9		10	7	1				4			12			2*		3	33
	2		8	3	5		7	11	9	6	12	1				4				10*					34
	2		11	5	6		8	9	10	3		1				4		7							35
	2		11*	5	6		8	9	10	3		1				4		7	12						36
	2	3		5	6		8	9	10	11		1				4		7							37
	2	3		5	6		8		10	11	7	1				4		9							38
	5*	2	9	3	4				7	6	10	1				8		11		12					39
	2	3	8	5	6				10	11	7	1				4		9							40
	2	3	9	5	6		8		10	11	7	1				4									41
	2	3	9*	5	6		8		10	11	7	1				4		12							42
25	40	32	27	40	38	8	40	31	38	33	30	17	3	1	1	24	2	12	4	12		2	1	1	
											6				2	1		1	4	2	2				
		3	4	3	5		7	12	3	1	5			1				1		1					

1983-84

1	Aug	27	(a)	Crystal Palace	W 2-0	May, Parlane	13,382
2		29	(a)	Cardiff C	L 1-2	Tolmie	8,899
3	Sep	3	(h)	Barnsley	W 3-2	Tolmie 2, Parlane	25,105
4		7	(h)	Fulham	D 0-0		23,356
5		10	(a)	Portsmouth	W 2-1	Parlane, Tolmie (pen)	18,852
6		17	(h)	Blackburn R	W 6-0	May, Parlane 3, Tolmie, Baker	25,433
7		24	(a)	Leeds U	W 2-1	Baker, Parlane	21,918
8	Oct	1	(h)	Grimsby T	W 2-1	Caton, Tolmie	25,080
9		8	(h)	Swansea C	W 2-1	Parlane, Davidson	23,571
10		15	(a)	Charlton Ath	L 0-1		7,639
11		22	(h)	Middlesbrough	W 2-1	Parlane, Tolmie	24,466
12		29	(a)	Newcastle U	L 0-5		33,588
13	Nov	5	(a)	Shrewsbury T	W 3-1	May, Caton, Kinsey	9,471
14		12	(h)	Brighton & H.A.	W 4-0	Baker 2, Tolmie, Parlane	24,562
15		19	(a)	Carlisle U	L 0-2		8,745
16		26	(h)	Derby Co	D 1-1	Parlane	22,689
17	Dec	3	(a)	Chelsea	W 1-0	Tolmie	29,142
18		10	(h)	Sheffield W	L 1-2	Bond	41,862
19		17	(a)	Cambridge U	D 0-0		5,204
20		26	(h)	Oldham Ath	W 2-0	Kinsey, Parlane	35,898
21		27	(a)	Huddersfield T	W 3-1	Kinsey, Baker, Lomax	23,497
22		31	(a)	Barnsley	D 1-1	Parlane	17,148
23	Jan	2	(h)	Leeds U	D 1-1	Tolmie (pen)	34,441
24		14	(h)	Crystal Palace	W 3-1	Power, Baker, Kinsey	20,144
25		21	(a)	Blackburn R	L 1-2	Tolmie (pen)	18,199
26	Feb	4	(a)	Grimsby T	D 1-1	Parlane	11,986
27		11	(h)	Portsmouth	W 2-1	Tolmie (pen), Reid	23,138
28		18	(h)	Newcastle U	L 1-2	Kinsey	41,767
29		25	(a)	Middlesbrough	D 0-0		9,343
30	Mar	3	(h)	Shrewsbury T	W 1-0	Reid	20,144
31		10	(a)	Brighton & H.A.	D 1-1	Hartford	14,132
32		17	(a)	Fulham	L 1-5	McNab	9,684
33		24	(h)	Cardiff C	W 2-1	Johnson, Baker	20,140
34		31	(h)	Charlton Ath	L 0-1		19,147
35	Apr	7	(a)	Swansea C	W 2-0	Parlane, Kinsey	6,261
36		14	(h)	Carlisle U	W 3-1	May, Smith, Parlane	20,760
37		20	(a)	Oldham Ath	D 2-2	McCarthy, Bond (pen)	20,320
38		23	(h)	Huddersfield T	L 2-3	Bond 2 (2 pens)	23,247
39		28	(a)	Derby Co	L 0-1		14,470
40	May	4	(h)	Chelsea	L 0-2		21,713
41		7	(a)	Sheffield W	D 0-0		36,763
42		12	(h)	Cambridge U	W 5-0	Tolmie, May, Baker, Kinsey, Power	20,787

FINAL LEAGUE POSITION: 4th in Division Two

Appearances

Sub. Appearances

Goals

Williams	Ranson	May	Bond	Power	Caton	McNab	Reid	Parlane	Hartford	Tolmie	Kinsey	Baker	Davies	Davidson	Walsh	Wilson	Hoyland	Lomax	Dalziel	McCarthy	Smith	Johnson	
1	2	3	4	5	6	7	8	9	10	11													1
1	2	3	4	5	6	7	8	9	10*	11	12												2
1	2	3	4	5	6	7	8	9		11		10											3
1	2	3	4	5	6	7	8	9		11		10											4
1	2	7	4	5	6		8	9		11		10	3										5
1	2	3	4	5	6	7	8	9*		11		10		12									6
1	2	8*		5	6	7	4	9		11		10	3	12									7
1	2	8		5	6	7	4	9		11		10	3										8
1	2	8*		5	6	7	4	9		11		10	3	12									9
1	2	8*		5	6	7	4	9		11		10	3	12									10
1	2	3		5	6	7		9		11		10		8	4								11
1	2	3		5	6	7		9		11	12	10		8*	4								12
1	2	3		5	6	7	4	9		11	8	10											13
1	2	8		5	6	7	4	9		11		10				3							14
1	2	8*	12	5	6	7	4	9		11		10				3							15
1	2*	8	4	5	6	7		9		11					12	3	10						16
1		3	4	5		7		9	10	11	12				6*			2	8				17
1	2	6	4	5		7		9	10	11	12							3	8*				18
1		3	4	5		7		9	10	11		8						2		6			19
1		3	4	5		7		9		11	10	8						2		6			20
1		3	4	5		7		9		11	10	8						2		6			21
1	12	3	4	5		7		9		11	10*	8						2		6			22
1		3	4	5		7		9		11		8						2	10	6			23
1		3	4	5		7		9		11	10	8						2		6			24
1		3	4	5		7		9		11	10	8						2		6			25
1		3	4	5		7		9		11	10	8						2		6			26
1		3	4	5		7	12	9*		11	10	8						2		6			27
1		3	4	5		7	2	9*		11	10	8						12		6			28
1	2	9	4	5		7	8	12		11*	10							3		6			29
1		3	4	5		7	2	9		11*	10	8							12	6			30
1		3	11	5			4		10		9	8						2	7	6			31
1		3	4	5		7	2	9	10	11		8								6			32
1	2	3*	4	5		7		9		12		10								6	8	11	33
1	2	3	4	5		7*		9		11	12	10								6		8	34
1		5	4					9		11	10	8				3		2		6	7		35
1		5	4					9		11*	10	8				3		2		6	7	12	36
1		5	4					9		12	10	8				3		2*		6	7	11	37
1	2	5	4					9		12	10	8				3				6	7	11*	38
1	2	5	4			10		9*		11	12	8				3				6	7		39
1	2	11*	4	6				9		7		8				3				6	10	12	40
1	2	7	4	5				9		11		8				3				6	10		41
1	2	7	4	5				9*		11	12	8				3				6	10		42
42	25	42	33	37	16	33	18	40	7	38	16	36	5	2	3	11	1	16	4	24	9	4	
	1		1				1	1		3	7			4	1			1	1			2	
		5	4	2	2	1	2	16	1	13	7	8		1				1		1	1	1	

1984-85

1	Aug	25	(a)	Wimbledon	D 2-2	Cunningham, Parlane	8,365
2		27	(h)	Grimsby T	W 3-0	Bond (pen), Smith	21,137
3	Sep	1	(h)	Fulham	L 2-3	Parlane 2	21,071
4		4	(a)	Wolverhampton W	L 0-2		13,255
5		8	(a)	Carlisle U	D 0-0		6,461
6		15	(h)	Huddersfield T	W 1-0	Baker	20,201
7		22	(a)	Cardiff C	W 3-0	Cunningham, Smith, Wilson	6,089
8		29	(h)	Crystal Palace	W 2-1	Kinsey, Smith	20,252
9	Oct	6	(h)	Oxford U	W 1-0	Kinsey	24,755
10		13	(a)	Shrewsbury T	L 0-1		8,563
11		20	(a)	Middlesbrough	L 1-2	Kinsey	7,737
12		27	(h)	Blackburn R	W 2-1	Lowey (og), May	23,798
13	Nov	3	(a)	Brighton & H.A.	D 0-0		14,034
14		10	(h)	Birmingham C	W 1-0	Phillips	25,369
15		17	(a)	Sheffield U	D 0-0		16,605
16		24	(h)	Portsmouth	D 2-2	Kinsey, Smith	23,700
17	Dec	1	(a)	Oldham Ath	W 2-0	Melrose, Smith	15,000
18		8	(h)	Notts Co	W 2-0	Melrose, Phillips	20,109
19		15	(a)	Charlton Ath	W 3-1	Melrose, Phillips, Smith	5,568
20		22	(a)	Fulham	L 2-3	Baker (pen), Melrose	6,748
21		26	(h)	Barnsley	D 1-1	Melrose	27,131
22		29	(h)	Wolverhampton W	W 4-0	Baker, Phillips, Smith, Wilson	22,022
23	Jan	1	(a)	Leeds U	D 1-1	Melrose	22,626
24		12	(a)	Huddersfield T	W 2-0	Smith, Wilson	15,640
25		19	(h)	Wimbleaon	W 3-0	Baker, Phillips, Smith	23,303
26	Feb	2	(a)	Crystal Palace	W 2-1	Phillips, Wilson	7,668
27		9	(h)	Carlisle U	L 1-3	Phillips	21,374
28		23	(h)	Brighton & H.A.	W 2-0	Phillips, Smith	20,227
29	Mar	2	(a)	Blackburn R	W 1-0	Kinsey	22,099
30		9	(h)	Middlesbrough	W 1-0	Phillips	22,399
31		16	(h)	Shrewsbury T	W 4-0	Kinsey, May, Power, Smith	20,828
32		19	(a)	Birmingham C	D 0-0		18,004
33		23	(a)	Oxford U	L 0-3		13,096
34		30	(h)	Cardiff C	D 2-2	Kinsey, Simpson	20,047
35	Apr	6	(a)	Barnsley	D 0-0		12,930
36		8	(h)	Leeds U	L 1-2	Tolmie	33,553
37		13	(a)	Grimsby T	L 1-4	Simpson	8,362
38		20	(h)	Sheffield U	W 2-0	Clements, Tolmie	21,132
39		27	(a)	Portsmouth	W 2-1	Phillips, Simpson	22,459
40	May	4	(h)	Oldham Ath	D 0-0		28,993
41		6	(a)	Notts Co	L 2-3	Simpson 2	17,812
42		1	(h)	Charlton Ath	W 5-1	May, Melrose, Phillips 2, Simpson	47,000

FINAL LEAGUE POSITION: 3rd in Division Two

Appearances

Sub. Appearances

Goals

Williams	Phillips	Power	Bond	McCarthy	Wilson	McNab	Baker	Cunningham	Smith	Tolmie	Parlane	May	Reid	Kinsey	Beckford	Melrose	Lomax	Simpson	Sinclair	McNaught	Clements	Hoyland	
1	2	3	4	5	6	7	8	9	10*	12	11												1
1	2	3	4	5	6	7	8	9	10*		11												2
1	2	3	6	5	4	7	8	9	10*	12	11												3
1	6	3		5	10	7*	8	9		12	11	2	4										4
1	7	3		5	6		8	9		10*	11	2	4	12									5
1	6	3		5	10		8	9	7		11*	2	4	12									6
1	6	3		5	10		8*	9	7	12		2	4	11									7
1	6	3		5	10		8	9*	7	12		2	4	11									8
1	6	3		5	10		8	9	7*	12		2	4	11									9
1	6	3		5	10	12	8	9*	7		11	2	4										10
1	6	3		5	10		8	9	7*			2	4	11	12								11
1	6	3		5	10		8	9	7			2	4	11									12
1	6	3		5	10		8*	9	7			2	4	11	12								13
1	6	3		5	10	8		9	7			2	4	11*		12							14
1	6	3			10	8		9	7			2	4			11*	2	12					15
1	6	3			10		8	9	12			2	4	11		7			2*				16
1	6	3		5	10		8		7			2	4	11		9							17
1	6	3		5	10		8		7			2	4	11		9							18
1	6	3		5	10		8		7			2	4	11		9							19
1	6	3		5	10		8		7			2	4	11		9							20
1	6	3		5	10		8	12	7*			2		11		9				4			21
1	6	3		5	10		8		7			2		11		9				4			22
1	6	3		5	10		8		7			2		11		9				4			23
1	6	3		5	10		8		7			2		11		9				4			24
1	6	3		5	10		8	12	7			2		11		9*				4			25
1	6	3		5	10		8		7			2		11		9				4			26
1	6	3		5*	10		8		7			2	12	11		9				4			27
1	6	3		5		10	8		7	11		2	4			9							28
1	6	3		5		10	8*		7	12		2	4	11		9							29
1	6	3		5		10			7			8	4	11		9					2		30
1	6	3		5		10			7	12		8*	4	11		9					2		31
1	6	3		5		10			7			8	4	11		9					2		32
1	6*	3		5		10			7	12		8	4	11		9					2		33
1	6	3		5		12				10		8*	4	11		9		7			2		34
1	6	10		5			8					2	4	11		9*	3	7			12		35
1	6	10		5			8*			12		2	4	11	9		3	7					36
1	6	10		5						9		3	8	11	12		2*	7			4		37
1	6	3		5		12				10		8	4	11		9*		7			2		38
1	6	3		5					10	9		8	4	11				7			2		39
1	6	3		5		10						8	4	11			12	7			2	9*	40
1	6	9		5		10						8	4	11			3	7			2		41
1	6	3				8				10		4		11		9	2	7			5		42
42	42	42	3	39	27	15	29	16	31	7	7	39	31	33	1	23	6	9	1	7	11	1	
						3		2	1	10			1	2	3	1	1	1			1		
	12	1	1		4		4	2	11	2	4	3		7		7		6			1		

1985-86

1	Aug	17	(a)	Coventry C	D 1-1	McIlroy	14,550
2		21	(h)	Leicester C	D 1-1	Lillis (pen)	25,528
3		24	(h)	Sheffield W	L 1-3	Simpson	26,934
4		26	(a)	W.B.A.	W 3-2	Lillis, Simpson, Wilson	12,122
5		31	(h)	Tottenham H	W 2-1	Simpson, Miller (og)	27,789
6	Sep	3	(a)	Birmingham C	L 0-1		11,706
7		7	(a)	Southampton	L 0-3		14,308
8		14	(h)	Manchester U	L 0-3		48,773
9		21	(h)	West Ham U	D 2-2	Lillis, Melrose	22,001
10		28	(a)	Oxford U	L 0-1		9,796
11	Oct	5	(h)	Chelsea	L 0-1		20,104
12		12	(a)	Watford	L 2-3	Lillis, McNab	15,418
13		19	(a)	Q.P.R.	D 0-0		13,471
14		26	(h)	Everton	D 1-1	Simpson	28,807
15	Nov	2	(a)	Arsenal	L 0-1		22,264
16		9	(h)	Ipswich T	D 1-1	Lillis (pen)	20,853
17		16	(a)	Nottingham F	W 2-0	Wilson, Simpson	15,140
18		23	(h)	Newcastle U	W 1-0	Lillis	25,179
19		30	(a)	Luton T	L 1-2	Lillis (pen)	10,096
20	Dec	7	(a)	Leicester C	D 1-1	Davies	10,289
21		14	(h)	Coventry C	W 5-1	Davies 2, Lillis, Simpson 2	20,075
22		21	(a)	Sheffield W	L 2-3	Lillis, McNab	23,177
23		26	(h)	Liverpool	W 1-0	Wilson	35,584
24		28	(h)	Birmingham C	D 1-1	McNab	24,955
25	Jan	1	(a)	Aston Villa	W 1-0	Lillis	14,215
26		11	(h)	Southampton	W 1-0	Phillips	21,674
27		18	(a)	Tottenham H	W 2-0	Davies, Lillis	17,009
28	Feb	1	(h)	W.B.A.	W 2-1	Power, Davies	20,540
29		8	(h)	Q.P.R.	W 2-0	Simpson, Davies	20,414
30		11	(a)	Everton	L 0-4		30,006
31	Mar	1	(h)	Oxford U	L 0-3		20,099
32		8	(a)	Chelsea	L 0-1		17,573
33		15	(h)	Watford	L 0-1		18,899
34		22	(a)	Manchester U	D 2-2	Wilson, Albiston (og)	51,274
35		29	(h)	Aston Villa	D 2-2	McNab, Wilson	20,935
36		31	(a)	Liverpool	L 0-2		4,316
37	Apr	5	(h)	Arsenal	L 0-1		19,590
38		12	(a)	Ipswich T	D 0-0		13,986
39		19	(h)	Nottingham F	L 1-2	Davies	19,715
40		26	(a)	Newcastle U	L 1-3	Davies	22,689
41		28	(a)	West Ham U	L 0-1		27,153
42	May	3	(h)	Luton T	D 1-1	Davies	20,361

FINAL LEAGUE POSITION: 15th in Division One

Appearances

Sub. Appearances

Goals

Williams	Phillips	Power	Clements	Johnson	Wilson	Lillis	McNab	Kinsey	McIlroy	Simpson	McCarthy	May	Tolmie	Beckford	Smith	Melrose	Nixon	Baker	Davies	Reid	Moulden	Redmond	Siddall	Barrett	
1	2	3	4	5	6	7	8	9	10	11															1
1	2	3	4		6	7	8	9	10	11	5														2
1	6*	3	4			7	8	9	10	11	5	2	12												3
1	6		4		3	7	8	9	10	11	5	2													4
1	6		4		3	7	8	9	10	11	5	2													5
1	6		4		3		8	9	10	11	5	2		7*	12										6
1	6		4		3	7	8	9	10*	11	5	2				12									7
1	6	8	4		3	7		9*	10	11	5	2				12									8
	6	8	4		3	7			10	11	5	2				9	1								9
	6	3	4		8	7		12	10*		5	2	11			9	1								10
	6	3	4		8	7	10			11	5	2	12			9*	1								11
	6	3	4			7	10			11	5	2					1	8	9						12
	6	11		4		7	10				5	3					1	8	9	2					13
	6	3	4			7	10			11	5						1	8	9	2					14
	6	8	4			7	10*			11	5	3				12	1		9	2					15
	6	8	4			7	10			11	5	3					1		9	2					16
	6	3	4		11	7	10			12	5	8					1		9*	2					17
	6	3	4		11	7	10			12	5	8					1		9*	2					18
	6	3		4	11*	7	10				5	8					1	12	9	2					19
	6	3	4			7	10			11	5	8*				12	1		9	2					20
	6	3	4			7	10			11	5*	8				12	1		9	2					21
	6	3	4		8	7*	10			11		5				12	1		9	2					22
	6	3	4		11		10				5	8				7	1		9	2					23
	6	3	4		11*	7	10			12	5	8					1		9	2					24
	6	3	4			7	10			11	5	8					1			2	9				25
	6	3	4			7	10			11	5	8					1		9	2					26
	6	3	4			7	10			11	5	8					1		9	2					27
	6	3	4			7	10			11	5	8					1		9	2					28
	6	3				7				11	5	8					1	10	9	2		4			29
	6	3				7	10			11	5	12					1	8*	9	2		4			30
	6	3	4	5		7	10			11							1	8	9	2					31
	6	3	4			7	10			11	5	8					1		9	2					32
	6	3	4			7	10			11	5	8					1		9*	2	12				33
	6	3	4*		11	7	10	9		12		8					1			2		5			34
	6*	3			11	7	10	9		12	5	8					1			2		4			35
	6	3			10	7		9		11	5	8								2		4	1		36
	6	3			10		8	9		11	5								7	2		4	1		37
		3			11	7	10				5	8		9				6		2		4	1		38
		3			12	7	10			11	5	8						6	9*	2		4	1		39
		3*			11	7	10			12	5	8						6	9	2		4	1		40
	2				6	7	10		8	11*	5	3		12					9	4			1		41
	6*				11	7	10		8	12	5	3					1		9	4				2	42
8	39	36	30	4	24	39	37	12	12	30	38	36	1	2		4	28	9	26	30	1	9	6	1	
					1			1		7		1	2	1	1	6		1			1				
	1	1			5	11	4		1	8						1			9						

1986-87

1	Aug	23	(h)	Wimbledon	W 3-1	Baker 2, Christie	20,756
2		25	(a)	Liverpool	D 0-0		39,989
3		30	(a)	Tottenham H	L 0-1		23,764
4	Sep	3	(h)	Norwich C	D 2-2	Christie 2	19,122
5		6	(h)	Coventry C	L 0-1		18,320
6		13	(a)	Oxford U	D 0-0		8,245
7		20	(h)	Q.P.R.	D 0-0		17,774
8		27	(a)	Luton T	L 0-1		9,371
9	Oct	4	(h)	Leicester C	L 1-2	Hopkins	18,033
10		11	(a)	Newcastle U	L 1-3	Simpson	21,780
11		18	(a)	Chelsea	L 1-2	Varadi	12,990
12		26	(h)	Manchester U	D 1-1	McCarthy	32,440
13	Nov	1	(a)	Southampton	W 1-1	Baker	14,352
14		8	(h)	Aston Villa	W 3-1	Moulden 2, Varadi	22,875
15		15	(h)	Charlton Ath	W 2-1	Moulden, Simpson	20,578
16		22	(a)	Arsenal	L 0-3		29,009
17		29	(h)	Everton	L 1-3	Moulden	27,097
18	Dec	6	(a)	Nottingham F	L 0-2		19,129
19		13	(h)	West Ham U	W 3-1	White, Varadi 2	19,067
20		21	(a)	Coventry C	D 2-2	Redmond 2	12,430
21		26	(h)	Sheffield W	W 1-0	Simpson	30,193
22		28	(a)	Charlton Ath	L 0-5		7,697
23	Jan	1	(a)	Watford	D 1-1	Varadi	15,514
24		3	(h)	Oxford U	W 1-0	McNab (pen)	20,724
25		17	(h)	Liverpool	L 0-1		35,336
26		24	(a)	Wimbledon	D 0-0		5,667
27	Feb	14	(a)	Norwich C	D 1-1	Brightwell	16,094
28		21	(h)	Luton T	D 1-1	Lake	17,507
29		28	(a)	Q.P.R.	L 0-1		12,739
30	Mar	7	(a)	Manchester U	L 0-2		48,619
31		14	(h)	Chelsea	L 1-2	McNab (pen)	19,819
32		21	(h)	Newcastle U	D 0-0		23,060
33		28	(a)	Leicester C	L 0-4		10,743
34	Apr	4	(a)	Aston Villa	D 0-0		18,241
35		11	(h)	Southampton	L 2-4	Stewart, Moulden	18,193
36		15	(h)	Tottenham H	D 1-1	McNab (pen)	21,460
37		18	(h)	Watford	L 1-2	McNab (pen)	18,541
38		20	(a)	Sheffield W	L 1-2	Varadi	19,769
39		25	(h)	Arsenal	W 3-0	Varadi 2, Stewart	18,072
40	May	2	(a)	Everton	D 0-0		37,541
41		4	(h)	Nottingham F	W 1-0	Varadi	21,405
42		9	(a)	West Ham U	L 0-2		18,413

FINAL LEAGUE POSITION: 21st in Division One

Appearances
Sub. Appearances
Goals

Suckling	May	Wilson	Clements	McCarthy	Redmond	Davies	McNab	Christie	Baker	Brightwell	Simpson	Barrett	Hopkins	Beckford	Moulden	White	Varadi	Gidman	Grealish	Reid	McIlroy	Barnes	Lake	Stewart	Langley	Nixon	
1	2	3	4	5	6	7	8	9	10	11*	12																1
1	2	3	4	5	6	7*	8	9		11	10	12															2
1	2*	3	4	5	6	7	8	9	12	11	10																3
1	2	3		5	6	10	8	9	4		11		7														4
1	3	11	2	5	6	10*	8	9	4	12			7														5
1	5	3	4		6		8	9		11		2	7	10													6
1	2	3	4	5	6		8*	9		10	11		7		12												7
1	2	3	4	5	6		8	9*			11		7	10		12											8
1	2	3		5	4		8	9			11		6		10	7											9
1	2	3	4	5	6		8			10	11		9			7											10
1	2	3	4	5	6		8		12	10	11*					7	9										11
1		3	4	5	6		8			12	11					7	9	2	10*								12
1		3	4	5			8		6		11				12	7*	9	2	10								13
1		3	4	5			8		7		11				10		9	2	6								14
1		3	4	5			8		7		11				10	12	9*	2	6								15
1		3	4	5			8		7		11				10	9		2	6								16
1		3	4	5			8		7		11*				10	9	12	2	6								17
1		3	4	5			8		7*						10	11	9	2	6	12							18
1		3	4	5	12		8				11				10	7	9	2	6*								19
1		3	4	5	6		8								10	7	9			2	11						20
1		3	4		6		8				11				10	7	9	2		5							21
1		3	4		6		8				11				10	7	9	2		5							22
1		3	4	5	6		8				11				10		9	2	7								23
1		3	4	5	6		8				11				10*	12	9	2	7								24
1		3	4	5	6		8							10		7	9	2				11					25
1	2	3	4	5	6		8				12			10*			9					11	7				26
1		3	4	5	6		8			7						12	9	2				11	10*				27
1		3	4	5	6		8			7					12		9	2				11	10*				28
1		3	4	5			8		6	7							9	2		10		11					29
1		3	4	5	12		8		7	6	11				10*		9			2							30
1		3	4	5			8		6*	12					10	7	9	2				11					31
1		3	4	5	11*		8				12					7	9	2	6					10			32
1		11		5	4		8				12					7	9	2*		3				10	6		33
1		3	4	5			8			11						7	9	2						10	6		34
1		3	4*	5			8				12				11	7	9	2						10	6		35
1		3	4	5			8				11						9	2				7		10	6		36
1	2	3	4	5			8				7				12		9					11*		10	6		37
		3	2	5	4		8		6*	12	11					7	9							10		1	38
	7	3	2	5	4		8				11						9							10	6	1	39
	7	3	2	5	4		8				11						9							10	6	1	40
	7	3	2	5	4		8				11						9							10	6	1	41
	7	3	2	5*	4		8				11				9	12								10	6	1	42
37	17	42	39	39	28	5	42	9	13	12	27	1	7	4	16	19	29	22	11	6	1	8	3	11	9	5	
					2				2	4	5	1			4	5	1			1							
				1	2		4	3	3	1	3		1		5	1	9						1	2			

1987-88

1	Aug	15	(h)	Plymouth Argyle	W 2-1	Stewart, Varadi	20,046
2		22	(a)	Oldham Ath	D 1-1	Varadi	15,984
3		31	(a)	Aston Villa	D 1-1	Scott	16,282
4	Sep	5	(h)	Blackburn R	L 1-2	Scott	20,372
5		12	(a)	Shrewsbury T	D 0-0		6,280
6		16	(h)	Millwall	W 4-0	Scott, Gidman, White, Stewart	15,430
7		19	(h)	Stoke C	W 3-0	Varadi 3	19,322
8		26	(a)	Leeds U	L 0-2		25,358
9		29	(a)	Hull C	L 1-3	Stewart (pen)	9,650
10	Oct	3	(h)	Leicester C	W 4-2	Stewart 2, Varadi 2	16,481
11		10	(h)	Sheffield U	L 2-3	White, Brightwell	18,377
12		17	(a)	Ipswich T	L 0-3		12,711
13		21	(a)	Bradford C	W 4-2	Stewart 2, Lake, White	14,818
14		24	(h)	Barnsley	D 1-1	Varadi	17,063
15		31	(a)	Swindon T	W 4-3	Varadi, White 2, Simpson	11,536
16	Nov	4	(h)	Middlesbrough	D 1-1	Hinchcliffe	18,434
17		7	(h)	Huddersfield T	W 10-1	McNab, Stewart 3, Adcock 3, White 3	19,583
18		14	(a)	Reading	W 2-0	Stewart 2	10,052
19		21	(h)	Birmingham C	W 3-0	Stewart, White 2	22,690
20		28	(a)	W.B.A.	D 1-1	Adcock	15,425
21	Dec	1	(a)	Bournemouth	W 2-0	White, Stewart	9,499
22		5	(h)	Crystal Palace	L 1-3	Lake	23,161
23		12	(a)	Millwall	W 1-0	Adcock	10,477
24		19	(h)	Oldham Ath	L 1-2	Stewart	22,518
25		26	(h)	Leeds U	L 1-2	White	30,153
26		28	(a)	Stoke C	W 3-1	Stewart 2, Brightwell	18,020
27	Jan	2	(h)	Shrewsbury T	L 1-3	Lake (pen)	21,455
28		16	(a)	Plymouth Argyle	L 2-3	Stewart, McNab	13,291
29		23	(h)	Aston Villa	L 0-2		24,668
30	Feb	6	(a)	Blackburn R	L 1-2	Varadi	13,508
31		13	(h)	Bournemouth	W 2-0	Varadi, Stewart	16,161
32		27	(a)	Leicester C	L 0-1		13,852
33	Mar	2	(h)	Hull C	W 2-0	Varadi 2	16,040
34		5	(h)	Ipswich T	W 2-0	Morley, Varadi	17,402
35		8	(a)	Sheffield U	W 2-1	Morley, White	13,906
36		19	(h)	Swindon T	D 1-1	Stewart	17,022
37		26	(a)	Barnsley	L 1-3	Varadi	9,061
38	Apr	2	(a)	Huddersfield T	L 0-1		7,835
39		4	(h)	Reading	W 2-0	Stewart 2 (1 pen)	15,172
40		9	(a)	Middlesbrough	L 1-2	Thompstone	19,443
41		23	(h)	Bradford C	D 2-2	Brightwell, Morley	20,335
42		30	(a)	Birmingham C	W 3-0	Brightwell 2, Varadi	8,014
43	May	2	(h)	W.B.A.	W 4-2	Morley, Stewart 2 (2 pens), Varadi	16,490
44		7	(a)	Crystal Palace	L 0-2		17,555

FINAL LEAGUE POSITION: 9th in Division Two

Appearances

Sub. Appearances

Goals

Nixon	Gidman	Hinchcliffe	Clements	Brightwell	Redmond	White	Stewart	Varadi	Scott	McNab	Adcock	Simpson	Lake	Mimms	Seagraves	Suckling	Morley	Stowell	Moulden	Beckford	Thompstone	Lennon	
1	2	3	4	5†	6	7	8	9	10*	11	12	14											1
1	2	3	4	5	6	7	8	9	10	11													2
1	2	3	4	5	6	7	8		10	11	9												3
1	2	3	4	5	6	7*	8		10	11	9	12											4
1	2	3		5*	6	7	8	9	10	11		12	4										5
1	2	3			6	7	8	9	10	11		5	4										6
1	2	3			6	7	8	9	10	11		5	4										7
	2	3			6	7	8	9	10	11†	14	5	4*	1	12								8
	2	3		11	6	7†	8	9	10	12		5*	14	1	4								9
	2	3		11	6	12	8	9	10*	7			5	1	4								10
1	2	3*	14	11	6	9	8		10	7		12	5		4†								11
1		3	4	5	6	2	8	12		7		10	9		11*								12
1	2	3	4	5	6	12	8	9		10		11	7*										13
1	2	3	4	5	6	12	8	9	7*	10		11											14
1	2	3	4	5	6	7	8	9		10		11*	12										15
1	2	3	4	5*	6	7	8	9†		10	14	11	12										16
1	2	3	4		6	7	8			10	9	11	5										17
1	2		4	3	6	7	8		12	10	9	11*	5										18
1	2	3	4		6	7	8			10	9	11	5										19
1	2	3	4	12	6	7	8	14		10*	9	11†	5										20
1	2	3	4		6	7	8	12		10	9*	11	5										21
1	2	3	4		6	7	8			10	9	11	5										22
1	2	3			6	7	8			10	9	11	5		4								23
	2	3	4		6	7*	8	12	10		9	11	5			1							24
		3	4	2	6	7	8	9	10			11	5			1							25
1		3	4	2	6	7	8	9*	12	10		11	5										26
1		3	4	2	6	7		9†	12	10	8	11*	5		14								27
1	2	3	4	5†	6	7	8	12		10	9*	14	11										28
1	2	3	4	5*	6	7	8	12				11	9				10						29
		3		2	6	7	8	9		4		11	5				10	1					30
	2	3			6	7	8	9	10	4		11	5					1					31
	2	3			6	7	8	9	10	5*		11			4		12	1					32
			2	3	6	7	8	9	10*	4		11	5				12	1					33
		3	2	4	6	7		9	10			11	5				8	1					34
		3	2*	4	6	7		9	10			11	5†		14		8	1	12				35
		3		2	6	7	8	9		10		11	4				5	1					36
		3		2	6	7†	8	9		10		11*	4		12		5	1	14				37
	2*	3		5	6	7	8	9				12	10†		4		11	1	14				38
	2	3		5	6	7	8			10		11			4		9	1					39
	2	3		5	6	7						11			4		10*	1	8	9	12		40
	14	3		5	6	7*	8			10			2†		4		9	1	12	11			41
		3		5	6	12	8	11		10					4		9	1		7		2*	42
		3		5	6	2	8	11		10					4		9	1		7			43
1		3		5*	6	2	8		12	10		14			4		9		11†	7			44
25	30	42	24	32	44	40	40	26	19	36	12	31	30	3	13	2	13	14	2	5		1	
	1		1	1		4		6	4	1	3	7	3		4		2		4		1		
	1	1		5		13	24	17	3	2	5	1	3				4				1		

1988-89

1	Aug	27	(a)	Hull C	L 0-1		11,653
2		29	(h)	Oldham Ath	L 1-4	Lake	22,594
3	Sep	3	(h)	Walsall	D 2-2	McNab (pen), Morley	17,104
4		10	(a)	Leeds U	D 1-1	McNab (pen)	23,122
5		17	(h)	Brighton & H.A.	W 2-1	Brightwell, Moulden	16,033
6		20	(a)	Chelsea	W 3-1	Brightwell 2, Moulden	8,858
7		24	(a)	Barnsley	W 2-1	White, Morley	9,300
8	Oct	1	(h)	Blackburn R	W 1-0	Biggins	22,111
9		5	(h)	Portsmouth	W 4-1	White, Moulden, Biggins, Lake	17,202
10		8	(a)	Ipswich T	L 0-1		15,521
11		15	(a)	Plymouth Argyle	W 1-0	Gayle	10,158
12		22	(h)	Birmingham C	D 0-0		20,205
13		26	(a)	W.B.A.	L 0-1		14,258
14		29	(h)	Sunderland	D 1-1	Hinchcliffe	22,398
15	Nov	5	(a)	Leicester C	D 0-0		14,080
16		12	(h)	Watford	W 3-1	Moulden, Biggins 2	21,142
17		19	(a)	Bournemouth	W 1-0	Moulden	9,874
18		26	(h)	Oxford U	W 2-1	Morley, Redmond	20,145
19	Dec	3	(a)	Crystal Palace	D 0-0		12,444
20		10	(h)	Bradford C	W 4-0	Brightwell 2, Moulden 2	20,129
21		17	(h)	Shrewsbury T	D 2-2	Hinchcliffe 2 (1 pen)	19,613
22		26	(a)	Stoke C	L 1-3	Gleghorn	24,056
23		31	(a)	Swindon T	W 2-1	Gayle, Beckford	10,776
24	Jan	2	(h)	Leeds U	D 0-0		33,034
25		14	(a)	Oldham Ath	W 1-0	Megson	19,200
26		21	(h)	Hull C	W 4-1	Biggins 2, Moulden, White	20,485
27	Feb	4	(a)	Portsmouth	W 1-0	Gleghorn	13,207
28		11	(h)	Ipswich T	W 4-0	Gayle, Biggins 2, Morley	22,145
29		18	(a)	Birmingham C	W 2-0	Gleghorn, McNab	11,707
30		25	(h)	Plymouth Argyle	W 2-0	McNab (pen), Biggins	22,451
31	Mar	1	(h)	W.B.A.	D 1-1	Moulden	25,109
32		4	(a)	Watford	L 0-1		15,747
33		11	(h)	Leicester C	W 4-2	Spearing (og), Morley 3	22,266
34		14	(a)	Sunderland	W 4-2	White 2, Gleghorn, Morley	16,101
35		18	(h)	Chelsea	L 2-3	McNab (pen), Taggart	40,070
36		25	(a)	Walsall	D 3-3	Oldfield, Moulden 2	7,562
37		27	(h)	Stoke C	W 2-1	Oldfield, Hinchcliffe (pen)	28,303
38	Apr	1	(a)	Brighton & H.A.	L 1-2	Morley	12,072
39		4	(a)	Shrewsbury T	W 1-0	Morley	8,271
40		8	(h)	Swindon T	W 2-1	Hinchcliffe (pen), Oldfield	22,663
41		15	(a)	Blackburn R	L 0-4		16,927
42		22	(h)	Barnsley	L 1-2	Lake	21,274
43		29	(a)	Oxford U	W 4-2	Gleghorn, White, Greenall (og), Brightwell	7,762
44	May	1	(h)	Crystal Palace	D 1-1	Gleghorn	33,456
45		6	(h)	Bournemouth	D 3-3	Moulden 2, Morley	30,564
46		13	(a)	Bradford C	D 1-1	Morley	12,479

FINAL LEAGUE POSITION: 2nd in Division Two

Appearances

Sub. Appearances

Goals

Dibble	Lake	Hinchcliffe	Gayle	Brightwell	Redmond	White	Biggins	Morley	McNab	Gleghorn	Varadi	Seagraves	Simpson	Moulden	Williams	Hughes	Beckford	Bradshaw	Megson	Taggart	Oldfield	Cooper	Scott	
1	2	3	4	5	6	7	8	9	10*	11	12													1
1	2	3	4	5	6	7†	8	9	10		12	14	11*											2
1	7	3	4	5	6	12		9	10	11†	8*	2		14										3
1	11	3	4	5	6	7		9	10			2		8										4
1	11	3	4	5	6	7		9	10			2		8										5
1	11	3	4	5	6	7		9	10			2		8										6
1	11	3	4	5	6	7		9	10			2		8										7
1	11	3	4		6	7	5	9	10			2		8										8
1	11	3	4		6	7	5	9	10			2		8										9
1	11	3	4		6	7	5	9	10			2*		8	12									10
1		3	4		6	7	5	9	10	2				8		11*	12							11
1	11	3	4	12	6	7	5	9	10	2†		14		8*										12
1		3	4	5	6	7	11	9*	10	2				8				12						13
1		3	4	5	6	7	11*		10	8		2					12	9						14
1		3	4	5	6	7	11	9	10			2		8										15
1		3	4	5	6	7	11	9	10			2		8										16
1		3	4	5	6	7	11	9	10			2		8										17
1	3†		4	5	6	7	11	9	10*	14		2		8			12							18
1	3*		4	5	6	7	11	9	10	14		2		8†				12						19
1	14	3	4	5	6	7*		9	10	11		2†		8			12							20
1	10	3	4	5	6	7	12	9		11*		2		8										21
1	10	3	4	5	6	7†	11*	9		8		2		14			12							22
1	8	3	4	5	6	7	11		10	12		2					9*							23
1	8*	3	4	5	6	7	11	12	10	14		2					9†							24
1	9	3	4	12	6	7	11		10	14		2		8†					5*					25
1	9	3	4		6	7	11		10			2		8					5					26
1	2		4		6	7	11	8	10	9									5	3				27
1	2		4		6	7	11	8	10	9									5	3				28
1	2		4		6	7	11	8	10	9									5	3				29
1	2	12	4		6	7	11†	8	10	9				14					5	3*				30
1	2	12	4		6	7	11	8	10	9†				14					5	3*				31
1	2	3	4		6	7	11	8	10	9*				12					5					32
1	2†	3	4		6		11*	8	10	9				7			12		5	14				33
1		3	4		6	7		8	10	9									5	2	11			34
1	2		4		6	7		8	10	9*				12					5	3	11			35
1*	2		4		6	7			10	9				8				12	5	3	11			36
	2	3	4		6	7		11	10	12				8					5		9*	1		37
	4	3		2*	6	7		11		12				8					5	14	9	1	10†	38
	2	3	4		6	7	11	8		9								12	5		10*	1		39
	2*	3	4		6	7	11	9	10					8					5		12	1		40
		3	4		6	7	11*	8	10					12					5	2	9	1		41
	2	3	4		6	7	12		10	11*				8					5		9	1		42
1	2	3		5	6	7		9	10	11				8					4					43
1*	2	3		5	6	7	14	9	10	11				8†					4		12			44
	2	3		5	6	7		9	10	11				8*					4		12	1		45
	2	3		5	6	7		9	10	11				8					4			1		46
38	37	37	41	24	46	44	29	39	42	25	1	21	1	29		1	2	1	22	9	8	8	1	
	1	2		2		1	3	1		7	2	2		7	1		6	4		2	3			
	3	5	3	6	1	6	9	12	5	6				13			1		1	1	3			

1989-90

1	Aug	19	(a)	Liverpool	L	1-3	Hinchcliffe	37,628
2		23	(h)	Southampton	L	1-2	Gleghorn	25,416
3		26	(h)	Tottenham H	D	1-1	White	32,004
4		30	(a)	Coventry C	L	1-2	White	16,111
5	Sep	9	(h)	Q.P.R.	W	1-0	Allen	23,420
6		16	(a)	Wimbledon	L	0-1		6,815
7		23	(h)	Manchester U	W	5-1	Oldfield 2, Morley, Bishop, Hinchcliffe	43,246
8		30	(h)	Luton T	W	3-1	Oldfield, Bishop, Brightwell	23,863
9	Oct	14	(a)	Arsenal	L	0-4		40,414
10		22	(h)	Aston Villa	L	0-2		23,354
11		28	(a)	Chelsea	D	1-1	Allen	21,917
12	Nov	4	(h)	Crystal Palace	W	3-0	White, Morley, Allen	23,768
13		11	(a)	Derby Co	L	0-6		19,239
14		18	(h)	Nottingham F	L	0-3		26,238
15		25	(a)	Charlton Ath	D	1-1	Allen	8,857
16	Dec	2	(h)	Liverpool	L	1-4	Allen (pen)	31,641
17		9	(a)	Southampton	L	1-2	Allen	15,832
18		17	(a)	Everton	D	0-0		21,737
19		26	(h)	Norwich C	W	1-0	Allen	29,534
20		30	(h)	Millwall	W	2-0	White 2	28,084
21	Jan	1	(a)	Sheffield W	L	0-2		28,756
22		13	(a)	Tottenham H	D	1-1	Hendry	26,384
23		20	(h)	Coventry C	W	1-0	White	24,345
24	Feb	3	(a)	Manchester U	D	1-1	Brightwell	40,274
25		10	(h)	Wimbledon	D	1-1	Hendry	24,126
26		24	(h)	Charlton Ath	L	1-2	White	24,030
27	Mar	3	(a)	Nottingham F	L	0-1		22,644
28		10	(h)	Arsenal	D	1-1	White	29,087
29		17	(a)	Luton T	D	1-1	Allen (pen)	9,765
30		21	(h)	Chelsea	D	1-1	Quinn	24,670
31	Apr	1	(a)	Aston Villa	W	2-1	Ward M, Reid	24,797
32		7	(a)	Millwall	D	1-1	Ward M	10,265
33		11	(a)	Q.P.R.	W	3-1	Allen, Hendry, Ward M	8,437
34		14	(h)	Sheffield W	W	2-1	Quinn, Heath	33,022
35		16	(a)	Norwich C	W	1-0	Heath	18,914
36		21	(h)	Everton	W	1-0	Quinn	32,144
37		28	(h)	Derby Co	L	0-1		29,542
38	May	5	(a)	Crystal Palace	D	2-2	Allen (pen), Quinn	20,056

FINAL LEAGUE POSITION: 14th in Division One

Appearances

Sub. Appearances

Goals

Dibble	Lake	Hinchcliffe	Bishop	Gayle	Redmond	Oldfield	Allen	Morley	McNab	Gleghorn	White	Fleming	Cooper	Brightwell	Beckford	Fashanu	Hendry	Seagraves	Taggart	Ward A	Harper	Reid	Megson	Ward M	Clarke	Heath	Quinn	
1	2	3	4	5	6	7*	8	9	10	11	12																	1
1	2	3	4†	5	6	7	8	9*	10	11	12	14																2
	11	3	4	5	6		8	9	10		7	2	1															3
		3	4	5	6		9	8	10		7	2	1	11														4
	11*	3	4	5	6		9	8	10		7	2	1	12														5
	11	3	4	5	6	8		9	10*		7	2	1	12														6
	11*	3	4	5	6	9		8			7	2	1	10	12													7
	11*	3	4	5	6	9		8	12		7	2	1	10														8
	11	3	4	5	6	9	12	8			7	2*	1	!0														9
1	11	3	4†	5	6	9	12	8			7	2		10*		14												10
1	11	3*	4	5	6	12	9	8	10		7	2																11
1	11	3	4	5	6		9	8	10		7	2																12
1		3	4	5	6	8	9		10		7	2*		11†	12	14												13
1		3	4		6	8	9		10		7	2			11		5											14
1		3	4	8	6	12	9*	11	10		7	2					5											15
1	11		4		6	12	9	8			7			10			5	2	3*									16
1	11	3	4		6	10*	9	8			7						5	2		12								17
1		3	14		6	12	9†	8*			7			11			5				2	4	10					18
1	11	3	8		6		12	9*			7			14			5				2	4	10†					19
1	11	3			6		9				7			12			5				2	4*	10	8				20
1	11	3			6	12	9*				7			14			5				2	4	10†	8				21
1	11	3			6		9*				7			14			5				2	4†	10	8	12			22
1	11	3			6						7			14	12		5				2*	4	10†	8	9			23
1	11	3			6						7			4	12		5				2		10	8	9*			24
1	11*	3			6		12				7			4			5				2		10	8	9			25
1	11	3			6*						7			14			5				2	4†	10	8	9	12		26
1	11	3			6						7			14			5				2	4†	10*	8	12	9		27
1	11	3			6		12				7						5				2	4	10	8*		9		28
1	4*	3			6		9				7			14			5				2		10†	8	12	11		29
1	3				6		9				7						5				2	4	11	8			10	30
1	2				6		9†				7			14			5				3	4	11	8		12	10*	31
1	2				6		9†				7			14			5				3	4	11*	8		12	10	32
1	2				6		9*				7			14			5				3	4	11	8		12	10†	33
1	2†				6		9*				7			14			5				3	4	11	8		12	10	34
1		14			6		9†							2			5				3	4	11	8	12	7	10*	35
1		14			6						7*			2			5				3	4	11†	8	12	9	10	36
1	11				6		12				7			2			5*				3	4		8		9	10	37
1	11	14			6		12				7*			2†			5				3	4		8		9	10	38
31	31	28	18	14	38	10	23	17	11	2	35	13	7	14	1		25	2	1		21	18	19	19	4	7	9	
		3	1			5	7		1		2	1		14	4	2				1					5	5		
		2	2			3	10	2		1	8			2			3					1		3		2	4	

1990-91

1	Aug	25	(a)	Tottenham H	L 1-3	Quinn	33,501
2	Sep	1	(h)	Everton	W 1-0	Heath	31,456
3		5	(h)	Aston Villa	W 2-1	Ward (pen), Pointon	30,199
4		8	(a)	Sheffield U	D 1-1	White	21,895
5		15	(h)	Norwich C	W 2-1	Quinn, Brennan	26,247
6		22	(a)	Chelsea	D 1-1	Ward (pen)	20,924
7		29	(a)	Wimbledon	D 1-1	Allen	6,158
8	Oct	6	(h)	Coventry C	W 2-0	Harper, Quinn	26,198
9		20	(a)	Derby Co	D 1-1	Ward (pen)	17,884
10		27	(h)	Manchester U	D 3-3	White 2, Hendry	36,427
11	Nov	3	(a)	Sunderland	D 1-1	White	23,137
12		10	(h)	Leeds U	L 2-3	Ward (pen), White	27,782
13		17	(a)	Luton T	D 2-2	White, Redmond	9,564
14		24	(a)	Liverpool	D 2-2	Ward (pen), Quinn	37,849
15	Dec	1	(h)	Q.P.R.	W 2-1	Quinn 2	25,080
16		15	(h)	Tottenham H	W 2-1	Redmond, Ward (pen)	31,263
17		22	(h)	Crystal Palace	L 0-2		25,321
18		26	(a)	Southampton	L 1-2	Quinn	16,029
19		29	(a)	Nottingham F	W 3-1	Quinn 2, Clarke	24,937
20	Jan	1	(h)	Arsenal	L 0-1		30,579
21		13	(a)	Everton	L 0-2		22,774
22		19	(h)	Sheffield U	W 2-0	Ward 2	25,741
23	Feb	2	(a)	Norwich C	W 2-1	Quinn, White	15,194
24		9	(h)	Chelsea	W 2-1	Megson, White	25,116
25	Mar	2	(a)	Q.P.R.	L 0-1		12,376
26		5	(h)	Luton T	W 3-0	Quinn 2, Allen (pen)	20,404
27		9	(h)	Liverpool	L 0-3		33,150
28		16	(h)	Wimbledon	D 1-1	Ward (pen)	21,089
29		23	(a)	Coventry C	L 1-3	Allen	13,198
30		30	(h)	Southampton	D 3-3	Allen, Brennan, White	23,163
31	Apr	1	(a)	Crystal Palace	W 3-1	Quinn 3	18,001
32		6	(h)	Nottingham F	W 3-1	Ward (pen), Quinn, Redmond	25,169
33		10	(a)	Leeds U	W 2-1	Hill, Quinn	28,757
34		17	(a)	Arsenal	D 2-2	Ward (pen), White	38,412
35		20	(h)	Derby Co	W 2-1	Quinn, White	24,037
36		23	(a)	Aston Villa	W 5-1	White 4, Brennan	24,168
37	May	4	(a)	Manchester U	L 0-1		45,286
38		11	(h)	Sunderland	W 3-2	Quinn 2, White	39,194

FINAL LEAGUE POSITION: 5th in Division One

Appearances

Sub. Appearances

Goals

Coton	Brightwell I	Pointon	Harper	Hendry	Lake	White	Reid	Quinn	Heath	Ward M	Redmond	Allen	Dibble	Brennan	Beckford	Megson	Clarke	Hill	Hughes	Margetson	
1	2	3	4	5*	6	7	8	9	10†	11	12	14									1
1	2	3	4	5	8	7	6	9	10	11											2
	2	3		5	8*	7	6	9	10	11	12		1	4							3
1	2	3	8	5		7	6	9*	10	11	4	12									4
1	2	3	8	5		7	6*	9	10	11	4†	12		14							5
1	2	3	8	5		7*	6†	9	10	11	4	12		14							6
1	2	3	4	5		7†		9	8*	11	6	12		10	14						7
1	2	3	10	5		7*	4†	9	8	11	6	12		14							8
1	14	3*	2	5		7	4	9†	8	11	6	12				10					9
1	12	3	2	5		7	4*	9	8	11	6					10					10
1		3	2	5		7	4	9	8	11*	6	12				10					11
1	14	3	2†	5		7	4*	9	8	11	6	12				10					12
1	2	3	4	5		7*		9	8	11	6			12		10					13
	2	3		5		7	4	9	8*	11	6	12	1			10					14
	2	3		5		7	4	9	8	11	6		1			10					15
1	2	3		5		7	4	9	8*	11	6					10	12				16
1	2*	3		5		7	4	9	8	11	6					10	12				17
1	2	3	12	5		7	4	9		11	6					10	8*				18
1	2	3		5		7	4	9	8*	11	6					10	12				19
1	2	3		5		7	4	9		11	6					10	8				20
1	2	3	12	5*		7	4	9	8	11	6	14				10†					21
1	2	3		5		7	4	9		11	6	8				10					22
1	2	3	4	5		7		9	12	11	6	8*				10					23
1	2	3	4	5		7		9	12	11	6	8*				10					24
1	2	3	12	5		7	4†	9	8	11*	6	14				10					25
1	2†	3	12	5		7	4*	9	11		6	8				10		14			26
1	2	3		5		7	4	9	12	11	6	8				10*					27
1	2		10	5		7	4	9	12	11	6	8*						3			28
1	2		10			7	4	9	5	11	6	8		3							29
1	2		10			7	4	9	5	11	6	8		3							30
1	2	3	10			7	4	9	5	11	6			8							31
1	2	3*	10			7	4	9	5	11	6			8					12		32
1	2	3	10			7		9	5	11	6			8				4			33
1	2	3	10			7		9	5	11	6			8				4			34
1		3	10	5		7	12	9	4	11*	6			8				2			35
1		3	10	5		7		9	4	11	6			8				2			36
		3	10	5		7	14	9	4	11*	6			8†			12	2		1	37
		3	10	5		7		9	4		6			8	12		11*	2		1	38
33	30	35	25	32	3	38	28	38	31	36	35	8	3	12		19	3	7		2	
	3		4				2		4		2	12		4	2		4	1	1		
		1	1	1		16		20	1	11	3	4		3		1	1	1			

1991-92

1	Aug	17	(a)	Coventry C	W	1-0	Quinn	18,013
2		21	(h)	Liverpool	W	2-1	White 2	37,322
3		24	(h)	Crystal Palace	W	3-2	Brennan 2 (2 pens), White	28,023
4		28	(a)	Norwich C	D	0-0		15,376
5		31	(a)	Arsenal	L	1-2	Brightwell I	35,009
6	Sep	4	(h)	Nottingham F	W	2-1	Quinn, Hill	29,146
7		7	(a)	Leeds U	L	0-3		29,986
8		14	(h)	Sheffield W	L	0-1		29,453
9		17	(h)	Everton	L	0-1		27,509
10		21	(a)	West Ham U	W	2-1	Redmond (pen), Hendry	25,588
11		28	(h)	Oldham Ath	L	1-2	White	31,271
12	Oct	6	(a)	Notts Co	W	3-1	Sheron, Allen C 2 (1 pen)	11,878
13		19	(a)	Tottenham H	W	1-0	Quinn	30,502
14		26	(h)	Sheffield U	W	3-2	Sheron, Quinn, Hughes	25,495
15	Nov	2	(a)	Southampton	W	3-0	Quinn, Sheron, Gittens (og)	13,933
16		16	(h)	Manchester U	D	0-0		38,180
17		23	(a)	Luton Town	D	2-2	Curle, Quinn	10,031
18		30	(h)	Wimbledon	D	0-0		22,429
19	Dec	7	(a)	Aston Villa	L	1-3	White	26,265
20		14	(h)	Q.P.R.	D	2-2	White, Curle	21,437
21		20	(a)	Liverpool	D	2-2	White 2	36,743
22		26	(h)	Norwich C	W	2-1	Quinn, White	28,164
23		28	(h)	Arsenal	W	1-0	White	32,325
24	Jan	1	(a)	Chelsea	D	1-1	Sheron	18,196
25		11	(a)	Crystal Palace	D	1-1	Curle (pen)	14,766
26		18	(h)	Coventry C	W	1-0	White	23,005
27	Feb	1	(h)	Tottenham H	W	1-0	White	30,123
28		8	(a)	Sheffield U	L	2-4	Curle (pen), Hill	26,562
29		15	(h)	Luton T	W	4-0	White 2, Hill, Heath	22,137
30		22	(a)	Wimbledon	L	1-2	Sheron	5,802
31		29	(h)	Aston Villa	W	2-0	Quinn, White	28,268
32	Mar	7	(a)	Q.P.R.	L	0-4		10,779
33		15	(h)	Southampton	L	0-1		24,265
34		21	(a)	Nottingham F	L	0-2		24,115
35		28	(h)	Chelsea	D	0-0		23,633
36	Apr	4	(h)	Leeds U	W	4-0	Hill, Sheron, Quinn, Brennan	30,239
37		7	(a)	Manchester U	D	1-1	Curle (pen)	46,781
38		11	(a)	Sheffield W	L	0-2		32,138
39		18	(h)	West Ham U	W	2-0	Pointon, Clarke W	25,601
40		20	(a)	Everton	W	2-1	Quinn 2	21,101
41		25	(h)	Notts Co	W	2-0	Simpson, Quinn	23,426
42	May	2	(a)	Oldham Ath	W	5-2	Mike, White 3, Sheron	18,588

FINAL LEAGUE POSITION: 5th in Division One

Appearances

Sub. Appearances

Goals

Margetson	Hill	Pointon	Reid	Curle	Redmond	White	Brightwell I	Quinn	Megson	Brennan	Heath	Coton	Hendry	Hughes	Sheron	Dibble	Allen C	Hoekman	Quigley	McMahon	Brightwell D	Simpson	Clarke W	Vonk	Mike	
1	2	3	4*	5	6	7	8	9	10	11	12															1
	2	3	4*	5	6	7	8	9	10	11	12	1														2
	2	3	4	5	6†	7	8	9	10*	11	12	1	14													3
	2	3	4	5	6	7	8		10	11	9	1														4
	2	3	4*	5	6	7	8	9	10	11†	12	1	14													5
	2	3	4	5	6	7	8	9	10	11		1														6
	2	3	4	5	6	7	8	9	10	11*	12	1														7
	2	3	4	5	6	7	8	9	10	11*	12	1														8
	2†	3	4*	5	6	7		9	10		8	1	14	11	12											9
	2	3		5	6	7	4	9	10		8	1	12	11*												10
	2†	3		5*	6	7	4	9	10		8		12	11	14	1										11
		3	4		6	7	9		10	2†	8	1		11*	5		12	14								12
	2	3	4	5	6		10	9			8	1		11	7											13
	2	3	4	5	6		10	9			8	1		11	7											14
	2	3	4	5	6		10	9*			8	1	12	11	7											15
	2	3	4†	5	6	7*	10	9			8	1		11	12		14									16
1	2	3		5	6	7*	10	9	4		8			11	12											17
	2†	3		5	6	7	10	9	4*		8	1		11	12		14									18
	2	3		5		7	10	9	4		8	1		11*	6				12							19
	2	3		5	6	7	10	9	4		8	1		11												20
		3	4	5	6	7	2	9			8	1		11	10											21
		3	4	5	6	7	2	9	12		8	1		11						10*						22
	2*	3	4	5	6	7	10	9	12		8	1		11												23
		3	4†	5	6	7	2	9	10		8*			11	12	1			14							24
		3	4*	5	6	7	2	9	10		8	1		11†	12				14							25
	2	3*	4	5	6	7	8					1		11	9				12	10						26
	2	3	4*	5	6	7	8					1		11	9				12	10						27
	2	3	4	5	6†	7	8	9	14		12	1		11*						10						28
	2	3	4*	5	6	7	8	9			12	1		11†	14					10						29
	2	3	4	5	6*	7	8†	9			11	1			14					10	12					30
	2	3	4	5		7	12	9				1		11*	8					10	6					31
	2	3	4	5		7		9			11	1			8*					10	6	12				32
	2	3	4*	5		7	14	9				1		11	8					10	6†	12				33
1	2		4*	5†	6	7	3	9							8					10		11	12	14		34
	2	3			6	7	4*			9		1			8					10		11	12	5		35
	2	3		5		7	12	9*		4		1			8					11		10		6		36
	2	3	14	5		7	12	9		4*		1			8†					11		10		6		37
	2	3	14	5		7	9			4†		1			8					11		10*	12	6		38
	2*	3		5		7	4					1		9	8					11		10	12	6		39
		3	4†	5		7	2	9	14			1			8*					11		10	12	6		40
	2			5		7	3	9				1			8					11		4		6	10	41
	2			5		7	3	9				1			8					11		4		6	10	42
3	36	39	29	40	31	39	36	35	18	13	20	37		24	20	2				18	3	9		8	2	
			2				4		4		8		6		9		3	1	5		1	2	5	1		
	4	1		5	1	18	1	12		3	1		1	1	7		2					1	1		1	

1992-93

1	Aug	17	(h)	Q.P.R.	D	1-1	White	24,471
2		19	(a)	Middlesbrough	L	0-2		15,369
3		22	(a)	Blackburn R	L	0-1		19,433
4		26	(h)	Norwich C	W	3-1	White 2, McMahon	23,182
5		29	(h)	Oldham Ath	D	3-3	Quinn, Vonk, White	27,288
6	Sep	1	(a)	Wimbledon	W	1-0	White	4,714
7		5	(a)	Sheffield W	W	3-0	White 2, Vonk	27,169
8		12	(h)	Middlesbrough	L	0-1		25,244
9		20	(h)	Chelsea	L	0-1		22,420
10		28	(a)	Arsenal	L	0-1		21,504
11	Oct	3	(h)	Nottingham F	D	2-2	Holden, Simpson	22,571
12		17	(a)	Crystal Palace	D	0-0		14,005
13		24	(h)	Southampton	W	1-0	Sheron	20,089
14		31	(a)	Everton	W	3-1	Sheron 2, White	20,242
15	Nov	7	(h)	Leeds U	W	4-0	Sheron, White, Hill, Brightwell I	27,255
16		21	(a)	Coventry C	W	3-2	Sheron, Quinn, Curle (pen)	14,590
17		28	(h)	Tottenham H	L	0-1		25,496
18	Dec	6	(a)	Manchester U	L	1-2	Quinn	35,408
19		12	(a)	Ipswich T	L	1-3	Flitcroft	16,833
20		19	(h)	Aston Villa	D	1-1	Flitcroft	23,525
21		26	(h)	Sheffield U	W	2-0	White 2	27,455
22		28	(a)	Liverpool	D	1-1	Quinn	43,037
23	Jan	9	(a)	Chelsea	W	4-2	White, Sheron 2, Sinclair (og)	15,939
24		16	(h)	Arsenal	L	0-1		25,041
25		26	(a)	Oldham Ath	W	1-0	Quinn	14,903
26		30	(h)	Blackburn R	W	3-2	Sheron, Curle (pen), White	29,122
27	Feb	6	(a)	Q.P.R.	D	1-1	Sheron	13,003
28		20	(a)	Norwich C	L	1-2	Sheron	16,386
29		23	(h)	Sheffield W	L	1-2	Quinn	23,619
30		27	(a)	Nottingham F	W	2-0	White, Flitcroft	25,956
31	Mar	10	(h)	Coventry C	W	1-0	Flitcroft	20,092
32		13	(a)	Leeds U	L	0-1		30,840
33		20	(h)	Manchester U	D	1-1	Quinn	37,136
34		24	(a)	Tottenham H	L	1-3	Sheron	27,247
35	Apr	3	(h)	Ipswich T	W	3-1	Quinn, Holden, Vonk	20,680
36		9	(a)	Sheffield U	D	1-1	Pemberton (og)	18,231
37		12	(h)	Liverpool	D	1-1	Flitcroft	28,098
38		18	(a)	Aston Villa	L	1-3	Quinn	33,108
39		21	(h)	Wimbledon	D	1-1	Holden	19,524
40	May	1	(a)	Southampton	W	1-0	White	11,830
41		5	(h)	Crystal Palace	D	0-0		21,167
42		8	(h)	Everton	L	2-5	White, Curle (pen)	25,180

FINAL LEAGUE POSITION: 9th in F.A. Premier League

Appearances

Sub. Appearances

Goals

Coton	Hill	Brightwell I	Simpson	Curle	Vonk	White	Lake	Quinn	Holden	McMahon	Sheron	Phelan	Reid	Flitcroft	Mike	Brightwell D	Ranson	Ingebritsen	Dibble	Quigley	Kerr	Margetson	
1	2	3	4	5	6	7	8*	9	10	11	12												1
1	2	3	4	5	6	7	8*	9	10	11	12												2
1	2	3	4	5	6	7		9	10	11	8												3
1		2	4	5	6	7		9	10	11	8	3											4
1		2	10	5	6	7		9*	10	11*	8†	3*	12	14									5
1		2	10	5	6	7		9	11	12		3	4*	8									6
1		2	10	5	6	7			11	12	9	3	4*	8									7
1		2	10	5	6*	7			11		9	3	4	8	12								8
1	6	2	10	5		7			11		9	3	4*	8	12								9
1	6	2	10	5		7		9	11*	12		3	4	8									10
1	6	2	10	5		7		9	11	4*	8	3	12										11
1	6	2	10	5		7		9	11	4		3		8									12
1	6	2	10	5		7		9	11	4	8	3											13
1	6	2	10*	5		7		9†	11	4	8	3	12	14									14
1	6	2	10	5		7		9	11	4	8	3											15
1	6	2*	10	5		7		9	11	4	8	3				12							16
1	6		10*	5		7		9	11	4	8	3		12		2							17
1	6	2	10*	5		7		9	11	4	8†	3	12	14									18
1	6*	2		5		7		9	11	4	12	3	8	10									19
1	6	2		5		7		9	11	4	12	3	8*	10									20
1	6	2		5		7		9	11	4	8	3		10									21
1	6	2		5		7		9	11	4	8*	3	12	10									22
1				5		7		9	11	4	8	3		10		6	2						23
1			4	5		7		9	11		8	3		10		6	2						24
1			6		5	7		9	11	4	8	3		10			2						25
1			10*	5	6	7		9	11	4	8	3					2	12					26
			10	5	6	7		9*	11	4†	8	3	14				2	12	1				27
1	12			5	6	7		9	11		8	3*		10			2	4†		14			28
1	3			5	6	7		9			8			10	11*	12	2			4			29
1	5		4		6	7		9	11		8*	3		10			2			12			30
1	2		4	5	6	7		9	11		8	3		10									31
1	2		4	5	6	7		9*	11		12	3		10			8						32
1	2			5	6	7		9	11		8	3	4	10									33
1	2			5	6	7*		9	11		8	3	4	10†				12		14			34
1				5	6	7*		9	11		8	3	4	10			2	12					35
1					6	7		9	11		8	3	4	10			2	5					36
1				5	6	7†		9	11		8*	3	4	10			2	12		14			37
1			8	5	6	7		9	11*			3	4	10		12	2						38
1			11	5	6	7		9	14		8	3	4†	10		12	2*						39
1			12	5	6	7		9	11*	4	8			10		3	2						40
1				5	6	7		9	11	4	8*	3		10			2				12		41
			12	5	6	7		9	11	4*	8	3		10			2		14			1†	42
40	23	21	27	39	26	42	2	39	40	24	33	37	14	28	1	4	17	2	1	1		1	
	1		2						1	3	5		6	4	2	4		5	1	4	1		
	1	1	1	3	3	16		9	3	1	11			5									

1993-94

1	Aug	14	(h)	Leeds U	D	1-1	Flitcroft	32,366
2		17	(a)	Everton	L	0-1		26,025
3		21	(a)	Tottenham H	L	0-1		24,535
4		24	(h)	Blackburn R	L	0-2		25,185
5		27	(h)	Coventry C	D	1-1	Sheron	21,537
6	Sep	1	(a)	Swindon T	W	3-1	Vonk, Quinn, Mike	16,067
7		11	(h)	Q.P.R.	W	3-0	Quinn, Sheron, Flitcroft	24,445
8		20	(a)	Wimbledon	L	0-1		8,533
9		25	(a)	Sheffield U	W	1-0	Sheron	20,067
10	Oct	4	(h)	Oldham Ath	D	1-1	Sheron	21,401
11		16	(a)	Arsenal	D	0-0		29,567
12		23	(h)	Liverpool	D	1-1	White	30,403
13	Nov	1	(a)	West Ham U	L	1-3	Curle (pen)	16,605
14		7	(h)	Manchester U	L	2-3	Quinn 2	35,155
15		20	(a)	Norwich C	D	1-1	Quinn	16,626
16		22	(a)	Chelsea	D	0-0		10,128
17		27	(h)	Sheffield W	L	1-3	Sheron	23,416
18	Dec	4	(a)	Leeds U	L	2-3	Sheron, Griffiths	33,820
19		8	(h)	Everton	W	1-0	Griffiths	20,513
20		11	(h)	Tottenham H	L	0-2		21,566
21		18	(a)	Blackburn R	L	0-2		19,479
22		28	(h)	Southampton	D	1-1	Phelan	24,712
23	Jan	1	(a)	Newcastle U	L	0-2		35,585
24		15	(h)	Arsenal	D	0-0		25,642
25		22	(a)	Liverpool	L	1-2	Griffiths	41,872
26	Feb	5	(h)	Ipswich T	W	2-1	Griffiths, Flitcroft	28,188
27		12	(h)	West Ham U	D	0-0		29,118
28		19	(a)	Coventry C	L	0-4		11,739
29		22	(a)	Aston Villa	D	0-0		19,254
30		25	(h)	Swindon T	W	2-1	Horlock (og), Rocastle	26,360
31	Mar	5	(a)	Q.P.R.	D	1-1	Rocastle	13,474
32		12	(h)	Wimbledon	L	0-1		23,981
33		19	(h)	Sheffield U	D	0-0		25,448
34		26	(a)	Oldham Ath	D	0-0		16,462
35		29	(a)	Ipswich T	D	2-2	Walsh, Rosler	12,871
36	Apr	2	(h)	Aston Villa	W	3-0	Beagrie, Walsh, Rosler	26,075
37		4	(a)	Southampton	W	1-0	Karl	16,377
38		9	(h)	Newcastle U	W	2-1	Walsh, Brightwell D	33,774
39		16	(h)	Norwich C	D	1-1	Rosler	28,020
40		23	(a)	Manchester U	L	0-2		44,333
41		30	(h)	Chelsea	D	2-2	Rosler, Walsh	33,594
42	May	7	(a)	Sheffield W	D	1-1	Rosler	33,589

FINAL LEAGUE POSITION: 16th in F.A. Premier League

Appearances

Sub. Appearances

Goals

Coton	Hill	Phelan	McMahon	Curle	Vonk	White	Sheron	Simpson	Flitcroft	Holden	Reid	Brightwell D	Groenendijk	Quinn	Mike	Edghill	Kernaghan	Lomas	Dibble	Griffiths	Ingebritsen	Kerr	Quigley	Rocastle	Shutt	Foster	Rosler	Walsh	Karl	Brightwell I	Beagrie	
1	2	3	4	5†	6	7	8	9*	10	11	12	14																				1
1	2	3	4		6	7	8		10	11	12	5	9*																			2
1	2	3	4*		6	7	8		10	11	9	5		12																		3
1	2†	3	4*	5	6		8		10	11	12	14	7	9																		4
1		3	4	5	6	7	8		10	11			2	9																		5
1			4	5	6	7†	8	12	10	11		3	2*	9	14																	6
1		3	4	5		7*	8		10	11		6	2	9	12																	7
1			4	5			8	7	10			3	11*	9	12	2	6															8
1			4	5			8			11		3	7	9		2	6	10														9
		3	4	5			8		10	11*			7†	9	12	2	6	14	1													10
1		3	4	5			8	7	10					9		2	6	11														11
1		3	4	5		7	8	11*	10					9		2	6	12														12
1		3	4	5	12	7	8†		10					9		2	6	11*		14												13
1		3	4	5	11	7	8		10					9		2	6															14
1		3	4	5		7	8*	10						9		2	6	11		12												15
1		3	4	5	2	7	8*	10						9			6	11		12												16
1		3	4	5	2	7	8	10						9*	12		6	11														17
1		3	4	5	2	7	8	9*							10		6†	11		12	14											18
1		3	4	5	6	7	8		10									11		9*	12	2										19
1		3		5	6	7	8*		10			12						11		9	14	2	4†									20
1		3		5	6	7	8									2	4	11		9	12		10*									21
1		3		5	10		8	12				6				2	4	11†		9*	14			7								22
1					10		8*	9				3				2	6	11			12			4	7	5						23
1		11			10		12		14			5*	6†			2	4	3		9	8			7								24
1		11			10				7			6				2	5	3		9	8			4								25
1		11		5	6		8		10							2		3		9				4	7							26
1		3	4	5*	6		8		10							2	12	14		9				7	11†							27
1		3	4		6		8	12							14	2	5	10*		9†				7	11							28
1	12	3*	4		6		8	9								2	5	10						7	11							29
	14	3	4		6		8	11	10*							2	5		1	9				7†	12							30
	11	3	4		6		8								12	2	5		1	9*				7			10					31
1	11†	3	4		6			9*							12	2	5							7			8	10	14			32
1	2	11	4		6							3					5			12				7			8*	10	9			33
1	2		4	5	6		12					3												7			9*	10		8	11	34
	2		4	5	6							3							1					7			9	10		8	11	35
	2		4	5	6		12					3							1					7			9*	10		8	11	36
	2		4	5	6		12					3							1					7†			9	10*	14	8	11	37
	2		4	5	6							3						12	1					7			9	10	8*		11	38
	2		4	5	6							3						12	1					7			9	10	8*		11	39
	2		4	5	6							3							1					7			9	10	8*	12	11	40
	2		4		6							3				5			1					7			9	10		8	11	41
		3	4		6*				12							2	5	14	1					7†			9	10		8	11	42
31	15	30	35	29	34	16	29	12	19	9	1	19	9	14	1	22	23	17	11	11	2	2	2	21	5	1	12	11	4	6	9	
	2				1		4	3	2		3	3		1	8		1	6		5	6				1				2	1		
		1		1	1	1	6		3			1		5	1					4				2			5	4	1		1	

1994-95

1	Aug	20	(a)	Arsenal	L 0-3		38,368
2		24	(h)	West Ham U	W 3-0	Walsh, Beagrie, Rosler	19,150
3		27	(h)	Everton	W 4-0	Rosler 2, Walsh 2	19,867
4		31	(a)	Chelsea	L 0-3		21,740
5	Sep	10	(h)	Crystal Palace	D 1-1	Walsh	19,971
6		17	(a)	Sheffield W	D 1-1	Walsh	26,585
7		24	(h)	Norwich C	W 2-0	Quinn, Rosler	21,031
8	Oct	1	(a)	Leeds U	L 0-2		30,938
9		8	(h)	Nottingham F	D 3-3	Quinn 2, Lomas	23,150
10		15	(a)	Q.P.R.	W 2-1	Flitcroft, Walsh	13,631
11		22	(h)	Tottenham H	W 5-2	Walsh 2, Quinn, Lomas, Flitcroft	25,473
12		29	(a)	Coventry C	L 0-1		15,802
13	Nov	5	(h)	Southampton	D 3-3	Walsh 2, Beagrie	21,589
14		10	(a)	Manchester U	L 0-5		43,738
15		20	(a)	Leicester C	W 1-0	Quinn	19,006
16		26	(h)	Wimbledon	W 2-0	Flitcroft, Rosler	21,131
17	Dec	3	(a)	Ipswich T	W 2-1	Flitcroft, Rosler	13,754
18		12	(h)	Arsenal	L 1-2	Simpson	20,500
19		17	(a)	West Ham U	L 0-3		17,286
20		26	(h)	Blackburn R	L 1-3	Quinn	23,387
21		28	(a)	Liverpool	L 0-2		38,122
22		31	(h)	Aston Villa	D 2-2	Rosler 2	22,513
23	Jan	2	(a)	Newcastle U	D 0-0		34,437
24		14	(h)	Coventry C	D 0-0		20,232
25		25	(h)	Leicester C	L 0-1		21,007
26	Feb	4	(a)	Southampton	D 2-2	Kernaghan, Flitcroft	14,902
27		11	(h)	Manchester U	L 0-3		26,368
28		22	(h)	Ipswich T	W 2-0	Quinn, Rosler	21,430
29		25	(h)	Leeds U	D 0-0		22,892
30	Mar	4	(a)	Norwich C	D 1-1	Simpson	16,266
31		8	(h)	Chelsea	L 1-2	Gaudino	21,880
32		15	(a)	Everton	D 1-1	Gaudino	28,485
33		18	(h)	Sheffield W	W 3-2	Rosler 2, Walsh	23,355
34		21	(a)	Wimbledon	L 0-2		5,268
35	Apr	1	(a)	Crystal Palace	L 1-2	Rosler	13,451
36		11	(a)	Tottenham H	L 1-2	Rosler	27,410
37		14	(h)	Liverpool	W 2-1	Summerbee, Gaudino	27,055
38		17	(a)	Blackburn R	W 3-2	Curle (pen), Rosler, Walsh	27,851
39		29	(h)	Newcastle U	D 0-0		27,389
40	May	3	(a)	Aston Villa	D 1-1	Rosler	30,133
41		6	(a)	Nottingham F	L 0-1		28,882
42		14	(h)	Q.P.R.	L 2-3	Quinn, Curle (pen)	27,850

FINAL LEAGUE POSITION: 17th in F.A. Premier League

Appearances

Sub. Appearances

Goals

Coton	Hill	Phelan	McMahon	Curle	Vonk	Summerbee	Walsh	Rosler	Flitcroft	Beagrie	Quinn	Brightwell I	Lomas	Edghill	Griffiths	Mike	Dibble	Tracey	Brightwell D	Kernaghan	Simpson	Kerr	Foster	Gaudino	Burridge	Thomas	
1	2	3	4	5	6	7	8*	9	10†	11	12	14															1
1		3†	4	5	6	7	8	9*	10	11	12	2	14														2
1			4	5	6	7	8	9	10	11*	12	2	3														3
1			4*	5	6	7	8	9	10	11	12	2	3														4
1		3	4	5	6	7	8		10	11	9	2															5
1	5		4		6	7	8	9*		11	12	3	10	2													6
1	12	3		5*		7	8	9†	4	11	10	6	14	2													7
1	2*	3	12		6	7			4	11	9	5	10		14	8†											8
	5	3				7	8		4	11	9	6	10	2			1										9
15	12	3		5		7°	8*		4	11	9	6	10	2			1										10
		3		5		7	8		4	11	9	6	10	2			1										11
	2	3			6	7	8		4	11	9	5	10					1									12
	2*	3			6	7	8		4	11	9	5	10			12		1									13
		3			6	7	8		4	11	9	5	10	2				1									14
	2			5		7	8	12	4	11	9*	6	10				1		3								15
	2†			5		7	8	12	4	11	9*	6	10				1		3	14							16
				5		7	8†	10	4	11	9	6*		2			1		3	12	14						17
				5		7	8	10	4	11†	9	6	3				1			12	14	2*					18
					12	7	8	11	4		9	6	10				1		3†	5		2*	14				19
		12				7		10	4	11	9	6	3				1			5			2*	8			20
		3			12	7	8	9	4	11		6	2				1			5				10*			21
		3				7	8	9	4	11		6	10				1			5			2				22
		3			6*	7	8	9	4	11			10				1			5	12		2				23
		3		5		2	8	9	10	11							1		6*	4	12			7			24
				5	6	2	8	9	10	11	12	4					1		3*					7			25
1°				5	6*	2	8	9	10	11		7					15		3	4				12			26
1				5		2	8	9	10	11*	12	6							3	4				7			27
1		3		5		2	8†	9	10*	11	12	6								4	14			7			28
1	2	3		5	6	7					10	8								4	11			9			29
1	12	3		5	6†	2	8				9	10			14					4	11			7*			30
1		3		5		2*	8	9		11	12	6								4	10			7			31
1		3		5	6		8	9*		11	10	2									4		12	7			32
1		3		5	6	2	8	9	10	11											4			7			33
1		3		5	6	12	8	9	10	11	14										4*		2	7†			34
1				5	6*	12	8	9	10	11									3	4			2	7			35
1	4	3		5		7	8	9	10		12			2									6	11*			36
1		3†		5		7	8*	9	4	12	10			2						14			6	11			37
1				5		7	8*	9	4	12	10			3						6	11		2				38
1°		3		5		7	8*	9	4	12	10			2						6	11†			14	15		39
		3*		5		7	8	9†	4	12	10			2						6	11			14	1		40
				5		2	8		10	11	9			3						4	6			7*	1	12	41
				5		7	8†	9	4		10			2						6	12		3	11*	1	14	42
22	10	26	6	31	19	39	39	29	37	33	24	29	18	14		1	14	3	9	18	10	2	9	17	3		
1	3	1	1		2	2		2		4	11	1	2		2	1	1			4	6		2	3	1	2	
				2		1	12	15	5	2	8		2							1	2			3			

1995-96

1	Aug	19	(h)	Tottenham H	D	1-1	Rosler	30,827
2		23	(a)	Coventry C	L	1-2	Rosler	16,568
3		26	(a)	Q.P.R.	L	0-1		14,212
4		30	(h)	Everton	L	0-2		28,432
5	Sep	10	(h)	Arsenal	L	0-1		23,984
6		16	(a)	Newcastle U	L	1-3	Creaney	36,501
7		23	(h)	Middlesbrough	L	0-1		25,865
8		30	(a)	Nottingham F	L	0-3		25,620
9	Oct	14	(a)	Manchester U	L	0-1		35,707
10		21	(h)	Leeds U	D	0-0		26,390
11		28	(a)	Liverpool	L	0-6		39,267
12	Nov	4	(h)	Bolton W	W	1-0	Summerbee	28,397
13		18	(a)	Sheffield W	D	1-1	Lomas	24,422
14		22	(h)	Wimbledon	W	1-0	Quinn	23,617
15		25	(h)	Aston Villa	W	1-0	Kinkladze	28,027
16	Dec	2	(a)	Leeds U	W	1-0	Creaney	33,249
17		9	(a)	Middlesbrough	L	1-4	Kinkladze	29,469
18		18	(h)	Nottingham F	D	1-1	Rosler	24,287
19		23	(h)	Chelsea	L	0-1		28,668
20		26	(a)	Blackburn R	L	0-2		28,915
21	Jan	1	(h)	West Ham U	W	2-1	Quinn 2	26,024
22		13	(a)	Tottenham H	L	0-1		31,438
23		20	(h)	Coventry C	D	1-1	Rosler	25,710
24		31	(a)	Southampton	D	1-1	Rosler	15,172
25	Feb	3	(h)	Q.P.R.	W	2-0	Clough, Symons	27,509
26		10	(a)	Everton	L	0-2		37,354
27		24	(h)	Newcastle U	D	3-3	Quinn 2, Rosler	31,115
28	Mar	2	(h)	Blackburn R	D	1-1	Lomas	29,078
29		5	(a)	Arsenal	L	1-3	Creaney	34,519
30		12	(a)	Chelsea	D	1-1	Clough	17,078
31		16	(h)	Southampton	W	2-1	Kinkladze 2	29,550
32		23	(a)	West Ham U	L	2-4	Quinn 2	24,017
33		30	(a)	Bolton W	D	1-1	Quinn	21,050
34	Apr	6	(h)	Manchester U	L	2-3	Kavelashvili, Rosler	29,688
35		8	(a)	Wimbledon	L	0-3		11,844
36		13	(h)	Sheffield W	W	1-0	Rosler	30,898
37		27	(a)	Aston Villa	W	1-0	Lomas	39,336
38	May	5	(h)	Liverpool	D	2-2	Rosler (pen), Symons	31,436

FINAL LEAGUE POSITION: 18th in Premier League

Appearances

Sub. Appearances

Goals

Immel	Edghill	Phelan	Lomas	Symons	Brightwell I	Summerbee	Walsh	Rosler	Flitcroft	Kinkladze	Quinn	Kernaghan	Foster	Brown	Ingram	Kerr	Curle	Beagrie	Creaney	Ekelund	Phillips	Frontzeck	Clough	Hiley	Mazzarelli	Kavelashvili					
1	2	3	4	5	6	7	8	9*	10	11	12																				1
1	2	3	4*	5	6†	7	8	9	10	11	12	13																			2
1		3	4†	5		7	8*	9	10	11	12	6	2	13																	3
1		3		5		7		9	10	11	8	12	2	6†	4*	13															4
1	2	3		5	6	7		9	10	11*	12						4	8													5
1	2	3	13	5	6	12		9	10†	7*							4	11	8												6
1	2	3	10	5	6	12		9		11*				7†			4	13	8												7
1			10	5	3	12		9		7			2	6			4	11	8*												8
1	2	3	6	5		12		9	10	7	8†						4	11*	13												9
1	2	3†	6	5	12	7		9	10*	11	8						4		13												10
1	2		6	5	3*	7		9	10	11†	8			13			4		12												11
1	3		6	5		7		9	10†	11	8		2*	13			4		12												12
1	2		6	5	3	7		9	10	11	8						4														13
1	2*		6	5	3	7		9	10	11	8						4		12												14
1	2		6	5	3	7		9	10	11	8						4														15
1	2*		6	5	3	7		9	10	11	8						4		12												16
1			6	5	2	7				11	9			8	3		4		10												17
1			10	5	2	7		9		11	8	6*		12	3		4														18
1				5	2	7		9*		11	8			6	3		4		10	12											19
1				5	3	2		9	10	11	8			6			4		12	7*											20
1			7	5	3	2		9†	10*	11	8			6			4			12	13										21
1			6	5		2		8	10	11	8			12	3		4			7*											22
1			7*	5	3	2		8	10	11	8			6			4				12										23
1			6	5	12	2		8	10	11	8†						4				13	3*	7								24
1			6*	5	12	2		8†	10	11							4		13		7	3	8								25
1			6	5		2		9	10		12			7†			4		13		11*	3	8								26
1			6	5		2		9		11	10			7			4						8	3							27
1			6	5		2		9	10	11	8*						4				12	3†	7	13							28
1			6	5		2*		9	10	11		4							8		12	3†	7	13							29
1			8	5	6	2*		9	10	11		4										3	7		12						30
1			8*	5	6	2		9	10	11	12						4					3†	7	13							31
1			10	5	6	2°		9*		11	12			7			4					3†	8	13	14						32
1			10	5	6	2				11	8			7			4					12	9	3*							33
1				5	6	2		12		11	8			7			4				13	3†	9			10*					34
1			6	5	2	7†		12		11	8*						4				13	3	9			10					35
1			6	5	2			9		11	12			7			4				13	3†	8			10*					36
1			10	5	6	2		9		11	8			3			4						7								37
1			10	5	6	2		9		11	8*			3			4				12		7†			13					38
38	13	9	32	38	26	33	3	34	25	37	24	4	4	16	5		32	4	6	2	2	11	15	2		3					
			1		3	4		2			8	2		5		1		1	9	2	9	1		4	2	1					
			3	2		1		9		4	8								3				2			1					

1996-97

1	Aug	16	(h)	Ipswich T	W 1-0	Lomas	29,129
2		20	(a)	Bolton W	L 0-1		18,257
3		24	(a)	Stoke C	L 1-2	Rosler	21,116
4	Sep	3	(h)	Charlton Ath	W 2-1	Rosler (pen), Creaney	25,963
5		7	(h)	Barnsley	L 1-2	Clough	26,464
6		10	(a)	Port Vale	W 2-0	Rosler, Dickov	10,770
7		14	(a)	Crystal Palace	L 1-3	Kavelashvili	17,638
8		21	(h)	Birmingham C	W 1-0	Kinkladze (pen)	26,757
9		28	(a)	Sheffield U	L 0-2		20,867
10	Oct	12	(a)	Q.P.R.	D 2-2	Brightwell, Kinkladze (pen)	16,265
11		15	(a)	Reading	L 0-2		11,724
12		19	(h)	Norwich C	W 2-1	Clough, Dickov	28,269
13		27	(h)	Wolverhampton W	L 0-1		27,296
14		29	(a)	Southend U	W 3-2	Rosler, Kinkladze 2 (1 pen)	8,707
15	Nov	2	(a)	Swindon T	L 0-2		14,374
16		13	(h)	Oxford U	L 2-3	Dickov, Brightwell	23,079
17		16	(a)	Portsmouth	L 1-2	Rodger	12,841
18		19	(h)	Huddersfield T	D 0-0		23,314
19		23	(h)	Tranmere R	L 1-2	Summerbee	26,531
20		27	(h)	W.B.A.	W 3-2	Rosler, Kinkladze 2 (2 pens)	24,200
21	Dec	1	(a)	Wolverhampton W	L 0-3		23,911
22		7	(h)	Bradford C	W 3-2	Kinkladze (pen), Dickov, Whitley	25,035
23		21	(a)	Oldham Ath	L 1-2	Kinkladze	12,992
24		26	(h)	Port Vale	L 0-1		30,344
25		28	(a)	Barnsley	L 0-2		17,159
26	Jan	11	(h)	Crystal Palace	D 1-1	Tuttle (og)	27,395
27		18	(a)	Huddersfield T	D 1-1	Lomas	18,358
28		29	(h)	Sheffield U	D 0-0		26,551
29	Feb	2	(a)	Oxford U	W 4-1	Gilchrist (og), Kinkladze 2, Rosler	8,824
30		8	(h)	Southend U	W 3-0	Rosler 2, Kinkladze	26,261
31		22	(h)	Swindon T	W 3-0	Horlock, Summerbee, Rosler	27,262
32	Mar	1	(a)	Bradford C	W 3-1	Rosler 2 (1 pen), Horlock	17,609
33		5	(h)	Portsmouth	D 1-1	Horlock	26,051
34		8	(h)	Oldham Ath	W 1-0	Rosler	30,729
35		11	(a)	Birmingham C	L 0-2		20,084
36		15	(a)	Grimsby T	D 1-1	Kavelashvili	8,732
37		18	(a)	Tranmere R	D 1-1	O'Brien (og)	12,019
38		22	(h)	Stoke C	W 2-0	Atkinson, Lomas	28,497
39	Apr	5	(a)	Charlton Ath	D 1-1	Brannan	15,000
40		9	(h)	Bolton W	L 1-2	Kinkladze	28,026
41		12	(a)	W.B.A.	W 3-1	Rosler 2, Horlock	20,087
42		16	(h)	Grimsby T	W 3-1	Atkinson, Summerbee 2	23,334
43		19	(h)	Q.P.R.	L 0-3		27,580
44		22	(a)	Ipswich T	L 0-1		15,824
45		25	(a)	Norwich C	D 0-0		14,080
46	May	3	(h)	Reading	W 3-2	Dickov, Rosler, Heaney	27,260

FINAL LEAGUE POSITION: 14th in Division One

Appearances

Sub. Appearances

Goals

Immel	Brightwell I	Frontzeck	Lomas	Symons	Brown	Summerbee	Phillips	Kavelashvili	Kinkladze	Rosler	Hiley	Creaney	Clough	Kernaghan	Dickov	Foster	Dibble	Whitley	Ingram	Crooks	Wassall	McGoldrick	Rodger	Margetson	Heaney	Wright	Beagrie	Beesley	Horlock	Greenacre	Brannan	Atkinson	
1	2	3	4	5	6	7	8*	9†	10	11	12	13																					1
1	2	3*	4	5	6	12	13	9	10	11	7		8†																				2
1	2		4	5	6*	7	12	9†	10	11			8	3	13																		3
1			4	5	6	7			10	11	3*	13	8	12†	9	2																	4
		3*	4	5		7	12		10	11		13	6		9†	2°	1	8	14														5
		3	4	5	2†			12	10	11*			7		9		1	8	6	13													6
	12†	3°	4	5	2*			13	10	11			7		9		1	8	6		14												7
		3	4	5		7			10	11			8		9*		1	12			6	2											8
			4		12	7		13	10	11			8*		9†	5	1		3		6	2											9
	2		4	5		7		12	10	11			8		9*		1				6	3											10
	2	12	4	5		7*		13	10	11			8		9†		1				6	3											11
	2		4	5		7			10*	11			8		9		1	12			6	3											12
		3†	4	5		2		12	10	11			8		9		1	7*	13		6												13
		3		5	12	7			10*	11			8		9		1	2	13		6		4†										14
		12		5		7		13	10	11†			8		9		1	4*			6	2	3										15
	4			5		7		12	10	11			8		9†		1	13			6	2*	3										16
	3		4	5		7		12	10	11°			8*		13			14			6	2†	9	1									17
	3		4	5		7		9*	10	11°			12		13			14			6	2	8†	1									18
	3	12	4°	5		7		11†	10	13			14		9			8			6	2*		1									19
	3		4	5		7			10	11					9*			12		2	6			1	8								20
	3		4	5		7			10	11			12		9*		15	8		2	6			1°									21
	6		4	5		7		12	10	11†					9*			14		13		2	3	1	8°								22
	6		4	5		7*		12	10	11					9			8†		14		2	3	1									23
	6		4	5	8	7†		12	10	11*		13			9			14				2	3°	1									24
	6		4	5	12	7			10	11								8		3		2*		1	9								25
	6		4	5		7		12	10	11		8†						13	3°	14		2		1	9*								26
	6		4	5		7			10	11								12	3	8*		2			9	1							27
	2		4	5		7			10	11				6					3			8			9*	1	12						28
	2*		4	5		7			10	11				6					3			8			12	1			9				29
			4	5		7			10	11								12	3	2					8*	1		6	9				30
	2		4	5		7				11					9*							8			10	1		6	3	12			31
	2		4	5		7				11					9†				12			8		1	10*			6	3	13			32
	2		4	5	12	7				11					9†				10*			8				1		6	3	13			33
	2		4	5		7				11					9				10*	12		8				1		6	3				34
	2		4	5		7		12		11					9*				10	13		8				1		6†	3				35
	2		4			7		9*	10	11				5								8				1			3	12	6		36
	2		4	5		7			10	11									9*			8			12	1			3		6		37
	2		4	5		7		12	10	11												3				1			9		6	8*	38
	2			5		7		12	10	11				4								3				1			9		6	8*	39
	2			5		7			10	11				9					4*			8				1			3		6	12	40
	2			5		7		12	10	11°			13	9					14			4†		1					3		6	8*	41
	2			5		7			10	11†			4	9*						12				1	13				3		6	8	42
	2			5		7			10	11*				9								4		1	12				3		6	8	43
	2			5		7		12	10											11		4		1	9*				3		6	8	44
	2			5		7							9*		12			10		11		4		1					3		6	8	45
	2			5		7				11			12		9*			8†		10		4		1	13				3		6		46
4	36	8	35	44	7	43	1	6	39	43	2	1	18	9	25	3	12	12	13	8	14	33	8	17	10	13		6	18		11	7	
	1	3			4	1	3	18		1	1	4	5	1	4		1	11	5	7	1				5		1			4		1	
	2		3			4		2	12	15		1	2		5			1					1		1				4		1	2	

1997-98

1	Aug	9	(h)	Portsmouth	D	2-2	Rosler, Wiekens	30,474
2		15	(a)	Sunderland	L	1-3	Kinkladze (pen)	38,894
3		22	(h)	Tranmere R	D	1-1	Horlock	26,336
4		30	(a)	Charlton A	L	1-2	Wiekens	14,009
5	Sep	3	(a)	Nottingham F	W	3-1	Brannan 2, Dickov	23,681
6		12	(a)	Bury	D	1-1	Morley	11,216
7		20	(h)	Norwich C	L	1-2	Bradbury	27,258
8		27	(h)	Swindon T	W	6-0	Kinkladze, Casper (og), Horlock, Dickov 2, Bradbury	26,646
9	Oct	4	(a)	Ipswich T	L	0-1		14,322
10		18	(h)	Reading	D	0-0		26,488
11		22	(h)	Stoke C	L	0-1		25,333
12		26	(a)	Queen's Park R	L	0-2		14,451
13		29	(h)	Crewe Alexandra	W	1-0	Greenacre	27,384
14	Nov	1	(a)	Oxford U	D	0-0		8,592
15		4	(h)	Port Vale	L	2-3	Wiekens, Dickov	24,554
16		7	(h)	Huddersfield T	L	0-1		24,425
17		15	(a)	Sheffield U	D	1-1	Horlock	23,780
18		22	(h)	Bradford C	W	1-0	Vaughan	29,746
19		29	(a)	Stockport Co	L	1-3	Brannan	11,351
20	Dec	2	(a)	West Bromwich A	W	1-0	Dickov	17,904
21		6	(h)	Wolverhampton W	L	0-1		28,999
22		13	(a)	Birmingham C	L	1-2	Shelia	21,014
23		20	(h)	Middlesbrough	W	2-0	Rosler (pen), Dickov	28,097
24		26	(a)	Crewe Alexandra	L	0-1		5,759
25		28	(h)	Nottingham F	L	2-3	Shelia, Dickov	31,839
26	Jan	10	(a)	Portsmouth	W	3-0	Russell, Kinkladze, Rosler	13,512
27		17	(h)	Sunderland	L	0-1		31,715
28		28	(h)	Charlton A	D	2-2	Dickov (pen), Symons	24,058
29		31	(a)	Tranmere R	D	0-0		12,830
30	Feb	7	(a)	Norwich C	D	0-0		15,274
31		14	(h)	Bury	L	0-1		28,885
32		18	(h)	Ipswich T	L	1-2	Symons	27,156
33		21	(a)	Swindon T	W	3-1	Rosler 2, Bradbury	12,280
34		24	(a)	Reading	L	0-3		11,513
35		28	(h)	West Bromwich A	W	1-0	Rosler	28,460
36	Mar	3	(a)	Huddersfield T	W	3-1	Wiekens, Briscoe, Tskhadadze	15,694
37		7	(h)	Oxford U	L	0-2		28,720
38		14	(a)	Port Vale	L	1-2	Wiekens	13,122
39		21	(h)	Sheffield U	D	0-0		28,496
40		28	(a)	Bradford C	L	1-2	Whitley Jeff	17,099
41	Apr	4	(h)	Stockport Co	W	4-1	Goater, Jobson, Bradbury 2	31,855
42		11	(a)	Wolverhampton W	D	2-2	Pollock, Horlock	24,458
43		13	(h)	Birmingham C	L	0-1		29,569
44		17	(a)	Middlesbrough	L	0-1		30,182
45		25	(h)	Queen's Park R	D	2-2	Kinkladze, Bradbury	32,040
46	May	3	(a)	Stoke C	W	5-2	Goater 2, Dickov, Bradbury, Horlock	26,664

FINAL LEAGUE POSITION: 22nd in Division One

Appearances

Sub. Appearances

Goals

	Brightwell	Vaughan	Wiekens	Symons	Beesley	Brannan	Horlock	Bradbury	Kinkladze	Rosler	Summerbee	Dickov	Kernaghan	Van Blerk	McGoldrick	Scully	Edghill	Morley	Conlon	Heaney	Wright	Whitley Jeff	Greenacre	Brown	Kelly	Creaney	Russell	Shelia	Whitley Jim	Crooks	Tskhadadze	Beardsley	Briscoe	Jobson	Pollock	Goater	Bishop	
	2	3	4	5	6*	7	8	9	10	11†	12	13																										1
	2	3	4	5		7*	8	9	10	11†	12		6	13																								2
	2	3	4	5	6	7	8	9	10	11*	12																											3
	2		4	5		7	8	9		11	10			3	6*	12																						4
	2		4	5		7	8	9	10*		11	12		3			6																					5
			4	5		11	8	9	10		7			3*		12	6	2																				6
	2		4	5		11*	8	9	10		7	12		3†		13	6																					7
	2		4	5	3	11	8	9	10†			7*				12	6		13																			8
	2		4	5†	3	11	8	9	10	12		7*				13	6																					9
	2		4†	5		7*	8		10		12	11		3	13		6			9																		10
	2			5		7*	8		10		12	11		3	4		6		13	9†																		11
	2*		3	5		7	8		10			11			4†		6					12	13	9														12
		2	3	5		7	8					11		13		14	6		12		1	4*	10°	9†														13
		2	3	5		7	8					11		9			6	12			1	4	10*															14
		2	3	5		7	8		10			11				4	6*	12	9		1																	15
		2	3	5		7	8		10			11				12	6°		13			4*		14	9†													16
		5	4	3		6*	8		10			12			8		2							13		9†	11											17
		3	6	5		7	8		10			9			4*		2							12			11											18
		3	6	5		7	8		10			9			4*		2							12			11											19
		3	6	5		7	8†		10*	12		9		13			2							4			11											20
		3	6	5		7				12		9		10*			2					8		4			11											21
	12		6	5		7				11		9		10			2							4*			8	3										22
			6	5		7			10	11		9					2				1			4			8	3										23
	12		6	5*		7			10	11		9		13			2				1			4†			8	3										24
	2	5†	6			7			10	11		9		13		12					1			4*			8	3										25
	2			5					10	11		9					6				1			4			8	3	7									26
	2		7*	5		12			10°	11		9		13			6		14		1			4			8	3†										27
	2			5				12	10	11*		9°		13			6				1			4			8†	3	7	14								28
	2			5				9*	10	11				12			6				1			4			8	3		7								29
	2			5				9	10*	11				12			6				1			4†			8		13	7	3							30
	2*			5	12			9		11				10			6		13		1						8		4†	7	3							31
				5	14			12	10	11							2†				1	7					8	4	6	13°	3	9*						32
			12	5				13	10°	11											1	2		8			9†	4*	7		6	14	3					33
	2†		4	5				9		11		12									1	13		8			14		7°		6	10*	3					34
			4	5	12			9		11											1	2		8					7*		6	10	3					35
			7	5				9†		11											1	2		8*			13	4	12		6	10	3					36
			7	5				9*		11		12									1	2		13			14	4°	8		6	10	3†					37
1			4	5		8†			10	11		12					3			9°		2		13			14		7*					6				38
1			10*	5		12		9†		11		13					3					2							7		6			4	8			39
1			12	5				13		11†							3					2					14		7		6°			4	8	9	10*	40
1		6	5					11									3					2							7					4	8	9	10	41
1		6	5				3	11*		12							2							13			14		7					4	8°	9	10†	42
1		6	5			12	3	11†		13							2							14					7					4*	8	9	10°	43
1		6		5		12	3	11		13°							2					4†		10*					7						8	9	14	44
1		6		5		4†	3	11	10*			12					2										13		7						8°	9	14	45
1		6	4	5		12	3	11	13			10°					2					14							7*						8	9†		46
28	19	19	35	42	4	27	25	23	29	23	4	21	1	10	6	1	36	1	1	3	18	14	2	18	1	1	17	12	17	3	10	5	5	6	8	7	4	
	2		2		3	5		4	1	6	5	9		9	1	8		2	6			3	1	8			7		2	2		1					2	
		1	5	2		3	5	7	4	6		9						1				1	1				1	2			1		1	1	1	3		

1973-74 SEASON

FIRST DIVISION

Leeds United	42	24	14	4	66	31	62
Liverpool	42	22	13	7	52	31	57
Derby County	42	17	14	11	52	42	48
Ipswich Town	42	18	11	13	67	58	47
Stoke City	42	15	16	11	54	42	46
Burnley	42	16	14	12	56	53	46
Everton	42	16	12	14	50	48	44
Queen's Pk. Rangers	42	13	17	12	56	52	43
Leicester City	42	13	16	13	51	41	42
Arsenal	42	14	14	14	49	51	42
Tottenham Hotspur	42	14	14	14	45	50	42
Wolverhampton Wns.	42	13	15	14	49	49	41
Sheffield United	42	14	12	16	44	49	40
Manchester City	**42**	**14**	**12**	**16**	**39**	**46**	**40**
Newcastle United	42	13	12	17	49	48	38
Coventry City	42	14	10	18	43	54	38
Chelsea	42	12	13	17	56	60	37
West Ham United	42	11	15	16	55	60	37
Birmingham City	42	12	13	17	52	64	37
Southampton	42	11	14	17	47	68	36
Manchester United	42	10	12	20	38	48	32
Norwich City	42	7	15	20	37	62	29

1974-75 SEASON

FIRST DIVISION

Derby County	42	21	11	10	67	49	53
Liverpool	42	20	11	11	60	39	51
Ipswich Town	42	23	5	14	66	44	51
Everton	42	16	18	8	56	42	50
Stoke City	42	17	15	10	64	48	49
Sheffield United	42	18	13	11	58	51	49
Middlesbrough	42	18	12	12	54	40	48
Manchester City	**42**	**18**	**10**	**14**	**54**	**54**	**46**
Leeds United	42	16	13	13	57	49	45
Burnley	42	17	11	14	68	67	45
Queen's Pk. Rangers	42	16	10	16	54	54	42
Wolverhampton Wns.	42	14	11	17	57	54	39
West Ham United	42	13	13	16	58	59	39
Coventry City	42	12	15	15	51	62	39
Newcastle United	42	15	9	18	59	72	39
Arsenal	42	13	11	18	47	49	37
Birmingham City	42	14	9	19	53	61	37
Leicester City	42	12	12	18	46	60	36
Tottenham Hotspur	42	13	8	21	52	63	34
Luton Town	42	11	11	20	47	65	33
Chelsea	42	9	15	18	42	72	33
Carlisle United	42	12	5	25	43	59	29

1975-76 SEASON

FIRST DIVISION

Liverpool	42	23	14	5	66	31	60
Queen's Pk. Rangers	42	24	11	7	67	33	59
Manchester United	42	23	10	10	68	42	56
Derby County	42	21	11	10	75	58	53
Leeds United	42	21	9	12	65	46	51
Ipswich Town	42	16	14	12	54	48	46
Leicester City	42	13	19	10	48	51	45
Manchester City	**42**	**16**	**12**	**15**	**64**	**46**	**43**
Tottenham Hotspur	42	14	15	13	63	63	43
Norwich City	42	16	10	16	58	58	42
Everton	42	15	12	15	60	66	42
Stoke City	42	15	11	16	48	50	41
Middlesbrough	42	15	10	17	46	45	40
Coventry City	42	13	14	15	47	57	40
Newcastle United	42	15	9	18	71	62	39
Aston Villa	42	11	17	14	51	59	39
Arsenal	42	13	10	19	47	53	36
West Ham United	42	13	10	19	48	71	36
Birmingham City	42	13	7	22	57	75	33
Wolverhampton Wns.	42	10	10	22	51	68	30
Burnley	42	9	10	23	43	66	28
Sheffield United	42	6	10	26	33	82	22

1976-77 SEASON

FIRST DIVISION

Liverpool	42	23	11	8	62	33	57
Manchester City	**42**	**21**	**14**	**7**	**60**	**34**	**56**
Ipswich Town	42	22	8	12	66	39	52
Aston Villa	42	22	7	13	76	50	51
Newcastle United	42	18	13	11	64	49	49
Manchester United	42	18	11	13	71	62	47
West Brom. Albion	42	16	13	13	62	56	45
Arsenal	42	16	11	15	64	59	43
Everton	42	14	14	14	62	64	42
Leeds United	42	15	12	15	48	51	42
Leicester City	42	12	18	12	47	60	42
Middlesbrough	42	14	13	15	40	45	41
Birmingham City	42	13	12	17	63	61	38
Queen's Pk. Rangers	42	13	12	17	47	52	38
Derby County	42	9	19	14	50	55	37
Norwich City	42	14	9	19	47	64	37
West Ham United	42	11	14	17	46	65	36
Bristol City	42	11	13	18	38	48	35
Coventry City	42	10	15	17	48	59	35
Sunderland	42	11	12	19	46	54	34
Stoke City	42	10	14	18	28	51	34
Tottenham Hotspur	42	12	9	21	48	72	33

1977-78 SEASON

FIRST DIVISION

Nottingham Forest	42	25	14	3	69	24	64
Liverpool	42	24	9	9	65	34	57
Everton	42	22	11	9	76	45	55
Manchester City	**42**	**20**	**12**	**10**	**74**	**51**	**52**
Arsenal	42	21	10	11	60	37	52
West Brom. Albion	42	18	14	10	62	53	50
Coventry City	42	18	12	12	75	62	48
Aston Villa	42	18	10	14	57	42	46
Leeds United	42	18	10	14	63	53	46
Manchester United	42	16	10	16	67	63	42
Birmingham City	42	16	9	17	55	60	41
Derby County	42	14	13	15	54	59	41
Norwich City	42	11	18	13	52	66	40
Middlesbrough	42	12	15	15	42	54	39
Wolverhampton Wns.	42	12	12	18	51	64	36
Chelsea	42	11	14	17	46	69	36
Bristol City	42	11	13	18	49	53	35
Ipswich Town	42	11	13	18	47	61	35
Queen's Pk. Rangers	42	9	15	18	47	64	33
West Ham United	42	12	8	22	52	69	32
Newcastle United	42	6	10	26	42	78	22
Leicester City	42	5	12	25	26	70	22

1978-79 SEASON

FIRST DIVISION

Liverpool	42	30	8	4	85	16	68
Nottingham Forest	42	21	18	3	61	26	60
West Brom. Albion	42	24	11	7	72	35	59
Everton	42	17	17	8	52	40	51
Leeds United	42	18	14	10	70	52	50
Ipswich Town	42	20	9	13	63	49	49
Arsenal	42	17	14	11	61	48	48
Aston Villa	42	15	16	11	59	49	46
Manchester United	42	15	15	12	60	63	45
Coventry City	42	14	16	12	58	68	44
Tottenham Hotspur	42	13	15	14	48	61	41
Middlesbrough	42	15	10	17	57	50	40
Bristol City	42	15	10	17	47	51	40
Southampton	42	12	16	14	47	53	40
Manchester City	**42**	**13**	**13**	**16**	**58**	**56**	**39**
Norwich City	42	7	23	12	51	57	37
Bolton Wanderers	42	12	11	19	54	75	35
Wolverhampton Wns.	42	13	8	21	44	68	34
Derby County	42	10	11	21	44	71	31
Queen's Pk. Rangers	42	6	13	23	45	73	25
Birmingham City	42	6	10	26	37	64	22
Chelsea	42	5	10	27	44	92	20

1979-80 SEASON

FIRST DIVISION

Liverpool	42	25	10	7	81	30	60
Manchester United	42	24	10	8	65	35	58
Ispwich	42	22	9	11	68	39	53
Arsenal	42	18	16	8	52	36	52
Nottingham Forest	42	20	8	14	63	43	48
Wolverhampton Wns.	42	19	9	14	58	47	47
Aston Villa	42	16	14	12	51	50	46
Southampton	42	18	9	15	65	53	45
Middlesbrough	42	16	12	14	50	44	44
West Brom. Albion	42	11	19	12	54	50	41
Leeds United	42	13	14	15	46	50	40
Norwich City	42	13	14	15	58	66	40
Crystal Palace	42	12	16	14	41	50	40
Tottenham Hotspur	42	15	10	17	52	62	40
Coventry City	42	16	7	19	56	66	39
Brighton & Hove Alb.	42	11	15	16	47	57	37
Manchester City	**42**	**12**	**13**	**17**	**43**	**66**	**37**
Stoke City	42	13	10	19	44	58	36
Everton	42	9	17	16	43	51	35
Bristol City	42	9	13	20	37	66	31
Derby County	42	11	8	23	47	67	30
Bolton Wanderers	42	5	15	22	38	73	25

1980-81 SEASON

FIRST DIVISION

Aston Villa	42	26	8	8	72	40	60
Ipswich Town	42	23	10	9	77	43	56
Arsenal	42	19	15	8	61	45	53
West Brom. Albion	42	20	12	10	60	42	52
Liverpool	42	17	17	8	62	46	51
Southampton	42	20	10	12	76	56	50
Nottingham Forest	42	19	12	11	62	45	50
Manchester United	42	15	18	9	51	36	48
Leeds United	42	17	10	15	39	47	44
Tottenham Hotspur	42	14	15	13	70	68	43
Stoke City	42	12	18	12	51	60	42
Manchester City	**42**	**14**	**11**	**17**	**56**	**59**	**39**
Birmingham City	42	13	12	17	50	61	38
Middlesbrough	42	16	5	21	53	61	37
Everton	42	13	10	19	55	58	36
Coventry City	42	13	10	19	48	68	36
Sunderland	42	14	7	21	58	53	35
Wolverhampton Wns.	42	13	9	20	47	55	35
Brighton & Hove Alb.	42	14	7	21	54	67	35
Norwich City	42	13	7	22	49	73	33
Leicester City	42	13	6	23	40	67	32
Crystal Palace	42	6	7	29	47	83	19

1981-82 SEASON

FIRST DIVISION

Liverpool	42	26	9	7	80	32	87
Ipswich Town	42	26	5	11	75	53	83
Manchester United	42	22	12	8	59	29	78
Tottenham Hotspur	42	20	11	11	67	48	71
Arsenal	42	20	11	11	48	37	71
Swansea City	42	21	6	15	58	51	69
Southampton	42	19	9	14	72	67	66
Everton	42	17	13	12	56	50	64
West Ham United	42	14	16	12	66	57	58
Manchester City	**42**	**15**	**13**	**14**	**49**	**50**	**58**
Aston Villa	42	15	12	15	55	53	57
Nottingham Forest	42	15	12	15	42	48	57
Brighton & Hove Alb.	42	13	13	16	43	52	52
Coventry City	42	13	11	18	56	62	50
Notts County	42	13	8	21	45	69	47
Birmingham City	42	10	14	18	53	61	44
West Brom. Albion	42	11	11	20	46	57	44
Stoke City	42	12	8	22	44	63	44
Sunderland	42	11	11	20	38	58	44
Leeds United	42	10	12	20	39	61	42
Wolverhampton Wns.	42	10	10	22	32	63	40
Middlesbrough	42	8	15	19	34	52	39

1982-83 SEASON

FIRST DIVISION

Liverpool	42	24	10	8	87	37	82
Watford	42	22	5	15	74	57	71
Manchester United	42	19	13	8	56	38	70
Tottenham Hotspur	42	20	9	13	65	50	69
Nottingham Forest	42	20	9	13	62	50	69
Aston Villa	42	21	5	16	62	50	68
Everton	42	18	10	14	66	48	64
West Ham United	42	20	4	18	68	62	64
Ipswich Town	42	15	13	14	64	50	58
Arsenal	42	16	10	16	58	56	58
West Brom. Albion	42	15	12	15	51	49	57
Southampton	42	15	12	15	54	58	57
Stoke City	42	16	9	17	53	64	57
Norwich City	42	14	12	16	52	58	54
Notts County	42	15	7	21	55	71	52
Sunderland	42	12	14	16	48	61	50
Birmingham City	42	12	15	16	40	55	50
Luton Town	42	12	13	17	65	84	49
Coventry City	42	13	9	20	48	59	48
Manchester City	**42**	**13**	**8**	**21**	**47**	**70**	**47**
Swansea City	42	10	11	21	51	69	41
Brighton & Hove Alb.	42	9	13	20	38	67	40

1983-84 SEASON

SECOND DIVISION

Chelsea	42	25	13	4	90	40	89
Sheffield Wednesday	42	26	10	6	72	34	89
Newcastle United	42	24	8	10	85	53	80
Manchester City	**42**	**20**	**10**	**12**	**66**	**48**	**70**
Grimsby Town	42	19	13	10	60	47	70
Blackburn Rovers	42	17	16	9	57	46	67
Carlisle United	42	16	16	10	48	41	64
Shrewsbury Town	42	17	10	15	49	53	61
Brighton & Hove Alb.	42	17	9	16	69	60	60
Leeds United	42	16	12	14	55	56	60
Fulham	42	15	12	15	60	53	57
Huddersfield Town	42	14	15	13	56	49	57
Charlton Athletic	42	16	9	17	53	64	57
Barnsley	42	15	7	20	57	53	52
Cardiff City	42	15	6	21	53	66	51
Portsmouth	42	14	7	21	73	64	49
Middlesbrough	42	12	13	17	41	47	49
Crystal Palace	42	12	11	19	42	52	47
Oldham Athletic	42	13	8	21	47	73	47
Derby County	42	11	9	22	36	72	42
Swansea City	42	7	8	27	36	85	29
Cambridge United	42	4	12	26	28	77	24

1984-85 SEASON

SECOND DIVISION

Oxford United	42	25	9	8	84	36	84
Birmingham City	42	25	7	10	59	33	82
Manchester City	**42**	**21**	**11**	**10**	**66**	**40**	**74**
Portsmouth	42	20	14	8	69	50	74
Blackburn Rovers	42	21	10	11	66	41	73
Brighton & Hove Alb.	42	20	12	10	58	34	72
Leeds United	42	19	12	11	66	43	69
Shrewsbury Town	42	18	11	13	66	53	65
Fulham	42	19	8	15	68	64	65
Grimsby Town	42	18	8	16	72	64	62
Barnsley	42	14	16	12	42	42	58
Wimbledon	42	16	10	16	71	75	58
Huddersfield Town	42	15	10	17	52	64	55
Oldham Athletic	42	15	8	19	49	67	53
Crystal Palace	42	12	12	18	46	65	48
Carlisle United	42	13	8	21	50	67	47
Charlton Athletic	42	11	12	19	51	63	45
Sheffield United	42	10	14	18	54	66	44
Middlesbrough	42	10	10	22	41	57	40
Notts County	42	10	7	25	45	73	37
Cardiff City	42	9	8	25	47	79	35
Wolverhampton Wns.	42	9	9	25	37	79	33

1985-86 SEASON

FIRST DIVISION

Liverpool	42	26	10	6	89	37	88
Everton	42	26	8	8	87	41	86
West Ham United	42	26	6	10	74	40	84
Manchester United	42	22	10	10	70	36	76
Sheffield Wednesday	42	21	10	11	63	54	73
Chelsea	42	20	11	11	57	56	71
Arsenal	42	20	9	13	49	47	69
Nottingham Forest	42	19	11	12	69	53	68
Luton Town	42	18	12	12	61	44	66
Tottenham Hotspur	42	19	8	15	74	52	65
Newcastle United	42	17	12	13	67	72	63
Watford	42	16	11	15	69	62	59
Queen's Pk. Rangers	42	15	7	20	53	64	52
Southampton	42	12	10	20	51	62	46
Manchester City	**42**	**11**	**12**	**19**	**43**	**57**	**45**
Aston Villa	42	10	14	18	51	67	44
Coventry City	42	11	10	21	48	71	43
Oxford United	42	10	12	20	62	80	42
Leicester City	42	10	12	20	54	76	42
Ipswich Town	42	11	8	23	32	55	41
Birmingham City	42	8	5	29	30	73	29
West Brom. Albion	42	4	12	26	35	89	24

1986-87 SEASON

FIRST DIVISION

Everton	42	26	8	8	76	31	86
Liverpool	42	23	8	11	72	42	77
Tottenham Hotspur	42	21	8	13	68	43	71
Arsenal	42	20	10	12	58	35	70
Norwich City	42	17	17	8	53	51	68
Wimbledon	42	19	9	14	57	50	66
Luton Town	42	18	12	12	47	45	66
Nottingham Forest	42	18	11	13	64	51	65
Watford	42	18	9	15	67	54	63
Coventry City	42	17	12	13	50	45	63
Manchester United	42	14	14	14	52	45	56
Southampton	42	14	10	18	69	68	52
Sheffield Wednesday	42	13	13	16	58	59	52
Chelsea	42	13	13	16	53	64	52
West Ham United	42	14	10	18	52	67	52
Queen's Pk. Rangers	42	13	11	18	48	64	50
Newcastle United	42	12	11	19	47	65	47
Oxford United	42	11	13	18	44	69	46
Charlton Athletic	42	11	11	20	45	55	44
Leicester City	42	11	9	22	54	76	42
Manchester City	**42**	**8**	**15**	**19**	**36**	**57**	**39**
Aston Villa	42	8	12	22	45	79	36

1987-88 SEASON

SECOND DIVISION

Millwall	44	25	7	12	72	52	82
Aston Villa	44	22	12	10	68	41	78
Middlesbrough	44	22	12	10	63	36	78
Bradford City	44	22	11	11	74	54	77
Blackburn Rovers	44	21	14	9	68	52	77
Crystal Palace	44	22	9	13	86	59	75
Leeds United	44	19	12	13	61	51	69
Ipswich Town	44	19	9	16	61	52	66
Manchester City	**44**	**19**	**8**	**17**	**80**	**60**	**65**
Oldham Athletic	44	18	11	15	72	64	65
Stoke City	44	17	11	16	50	57	62
Swindon Town	44	16	11	17	73	60	59
Leicester City	44	16	11	17	62	61	59
Barnsley	44	15	12	17	61	62	57
Hull City	44	14	15	15	54	60	57
Plymouth Argyle	44	16	8	20	65	67	56
Bournemouth	44	13	10	21	56	68	49
Shrewsbury Town	44	11	16	17	42	54	49
Birmingham City	44	11	15	18	41	66	48
West Brom. Albion	44	12	11	21	50	69	47
Sheffield United	44	13	7	24	45	74	46
Reading	44	10	12	22	44	70	42
Huddersfield Town	44	6	10	28	41	100	28

1988-89 SEASON

SECOND DIVISION

Chelsea	46	29	12	5	96	50	99
Manchester City	**46**	**23**	**13**	**10**	**77**	**53**	**82**
Crystal Palace	46	23	12	11	71	49	81
Watford	46	22	12	12	74	48	78
Blackburn Rovers	46	22	11	13	74	59	77
Swindon Town	46	20	16	10	68	53	76
Barnsley	46	20	14	12	66	58	74
Ipswich Town	46	22	7	17	71	61	73
West Brom. Albion	46	18	18	10	65	41	72
Leeds United	46	17	16	13	59	50	67
Sunderland	46	16	15	15	60	60	63
Bournemouth	46	18	8	20	53	62	62
Stoke City	46	15	14	17	57	72	59
Bradford City	46	13	17	16	52	59	56
Leicester City	46	13	16	17	56	63	55
Oldham Athletic	46	11	21	14	75	72	54
Oxford United	46	14	12	20	62	70	54
Plymouth Argyle	46	14	12	20	55	66	54
Brighton & Hove Alb.	46	14	9	23	57	66	51
Portsmouth	46	13	12	21	53	62	51
Hull City	46	11	14	21	52	68	47
Shrewsbury Town	46	8	18	20	40	67	42
Birmingham City	46	8	11	27	31	76	35
Walsall	46	5	16	25	41	80	31

1989-90 SEASON

FIRST DIVISION

Liverpool	38	23	10	5	78	37	79
Aston Villa	38	21	7	10	57	38	70
Tottenham Hotspur	38	19	6	13	59	47	63
Arsenal	38	18	8	12	54	38	62
Chelsea	38	16	12	10	58	50	60
Everton	38	17	8	13	51	33	59
Southampton	38	15	10	13	71	63	55
Wimbledon	38	13	16	9	47	40	55
Nottingham Forest	38	15	9	14	55	47	54
Norwich City	38	13	14	11	44	42	53
Queen's Pk. Rangers	38	13	11	14	45	44	50
Coventry City	38	14	7	17	39	59	49
Manchester United	38	13	9	16	46	47	48
Manchester City	**38**	**12**	**12**	**14**	**43**	**52**	**48**
Crystal Palace	38	13	9	16	42	66	48
Derby County	38	13	7	18	43	40	46
Luton Town	38	10	13	15	43	57	43
Sheffield Wednesday	38	11	10	17	35	51	43
Charlton Athletic	38	7	9	22	31	57	30
Millwall	38	5	11	22	39	65	26

1990-91 SEASON

FIRST DIVISION

Arsenal	38	24	13	1	74	18	83
Liverpool	38	23	7	8	77	40	76
Crystal Palace	38	20	9	9	50	41	69
Leeds United	38	19	7	12	65	47	64
Manchester City	**38**	**17**	**11**	**10**	**64**	**53**	**62**
Manchester United	38	16	12	10	58	45	59
Wimbledon	38	14	14	10	53	46	56
Nottingham Forest	38	14	12	12	65	50	54
Everton	38	13	12	13	50	46	51
Tottenham	38	11	16	11	51	50	49
Chelsea	38	13	10	15	58	69	49
Queen's Pk. Rangers	38	12	10	16	44	53	46
Sheffield United	38	13	7	18	36	55	46
Southampton	38	12	9	17	58	69	45
Norwich City	38	13	6	19	41	64	45
Coventry City	38	11	11	16	42	49	44
Aston Villa	38	9	14	15	46	58	41
Luton Town	38	10	7	21	42	61	37
Sunderland	38	8	10	20	38	60	34
Derby County	38	5	9	24	37	75	24

Arsenal 2 points deducted
Manchester United 1 point deducted

1991-92 SEASON

FIRST DIVISION

Leeds United	42	22	16	4	74	37	82
Manchester United	42	21	15	6	63	33	78
Sheffield Wednesday	42	21	12	9	62	49	75
Arsenal	42	19	15	8	81	46	72
Manchester City	**42**	**20**	**10**	**12**	**61**	**48**	**70**
Liverpool	42	16	16	10	47	40	64
Aston Villa	42	17	9	16	48	44	60
Nottingham Forest	42	16	11	15	60	58	59
Sheffield United	42	16	9	17	65	63	57
Crystal Palace	42	14	15	13	53	61	57
Queen's Pk. Rangers	42	12	18	12	48	47	54
Everton	42	13	14	15	52	51	53
Wimbledon	42	13	14	15	53	53	53
Chelsea	42	13	14	15	50	60	53
Tottenham	42	15	7	20	58	63	52
Southampton	42	14	10	18	39	55	52
Oldham Athletic	42	14	9	19	63	67	51
Norwich City	42	11	12	19	47	63	45
Coventry City	42	11	11	20	35	44	44
Luton Town	42	10	12	20	38	71	42
Notts County	42	10	10	22	40	62	40
West Ham United	42	9	11	22	37	59	38

1992-93 SEASON

F.A. PREMIER LEAGUE

Manchester United	42	24	12	6	67	31	84
Aston Villa	42	21	11	10	57	40	74
Norwich City	42	21	9	12	61	65	72
Blackburn Rovers	42	20	11	11	68	46	71
Queen's Pk. Rangers	42	17	12	13	63	55	63
Liverpool	42	16	11	15	62	55	59
Sheffield Wednesday	42	15	14	13	55	51	59
Tottenham	42	16	11	15	60	66	59
Manchester City	**42**	**15**	**12**	**15**	**56**	**51**	**57**
Arsenal	42	15	11	16	40	38	56
Chelsea	42	14	14	14	51	54	56
Wimbledon	42	14	12	16	56	55	54
Everton	42	15	8	19	53	55	53
Sheffield United	42	14	10	18	54	53	52
Coventry City	42	13	13	16	52	57	52
Ipswich Town	42	12	16	14	50	55	52
Leeds United	42	12	15	15	57	62	51
Southampton	42	13	11	18	54	61	50
Oldham Athletic	42	13	10	19	63	74	49
Crystal Palace	42	11	16	15	48	61	49
Middlesbrough	42	11	11	20	54	75	44
Nottingham Forest	42	10	10	22	41	62	40

1993-94 SEASON

F.A. PREMIER LEAGUE

Manchester United	42	27	11	4	80	38	92
Blackburn Rovers	42	25	9	8	63	36	84
Newcastle United	42	23	8	11	82	41	77
Arsenal	42	18	17	7	53	28	71
Leeds United	42	18	16	8	65	39	70
Wimbledon	42	18	11	13	56	53	65
Sheffield Wednesday	42	16	16	10	76	54	64
Liverpool	42	17	9	16	59	55	60
Queen's Pk. Rangers	42	16	12	14	62	64	60
Aston Villa	42	15	12	15	46	50	57
Coventry City	42	14	14	14	43	45	56
Norwich City	42	12	17	13	65	61	53
West Ham United	42	13	13	16	47	58	52
Chelsea	42	13	12	17	49	53	51
Tottenham Hotspur	42	11	12	19	54	59	45
Manchester City	**42**	**9**	**18**	**15**	**38**	**49**	**45**
Everton	42	12	8	22	42	63	44
Southampton	42	12	7	23	49	66	43
Ipswich Town	42	9	16	17	35	58	43
Sheffield United	42	8	18	16	42	60	42
Oldham Athletic	42	9	13	20	42	68	40
Swindon Town	42	5	15	22	47	100	30

1994-95 SEASON

F.A. PREMIER LEAGUE

Blackburn Rovers	42	27	8	7	80	39	89
Manchester United	42	26	10	6	77	28	88
Nottingham Forest	42	22	11	9	72	43	77
Liverpool	42	21	11	10	65	37	74
Leeds United	42	20	13	9	59	38	63
Newcastle United	42	20	12	10	67	47	72
Tottenham Hotspur	42	16	14	12	66	58	62
Queen's Pk. Rangers	42	17	9	16	61	59	60
Wimbledon	42	15	11	16	48	65	56
Southampton	42	12	18	12	61	63	54
Chelsea	42	13	15	14	50	55	54
Arsenal	42	13	12	17	52	49	51
Sheffield Wednesday	42	13	12	17	49	57	51
West Ham United	42	13	11	18	44	48	50
Everton	42	11	17	14	44	51	50
Coventry City	42	12	14	16	44	62	50
Manchester City	**42**	**12**	**13**	**17**	**53**	**64**	**49**
Aston Villa	42	11	15	16	51	56	48
Crystal Palace	42	11	12	19	34	49	45
Norwich City	42	10	13	19	37	54	43
Leicester City	42	6	11	25	45	80	29
Ipswich Town	42	7	6	29	36	93	27

1995-96 SEASON

F.A. PREMIER LEAGUE

Manchester United	38	25	7	6	73	35	82
Newcastle United	38	24	6	8	66	37	78
Liverpool	38	20	11	7	70	34	71
Aston Villa	38	18	9	11	52	35	63
Arsenal	38	17	12	9	49	32	63
Everton	38	17	10	11	64	44	61
Blackburn Rovers	38	18	7	13	61	47	61
Tottenham Hotspur	38	16	13	9	50	38	61
Nottingham Forest	38	15	13	10	50	54	58
West Ham United	38	14	9	15	43	52	51
Chelsea	38	12	14	12	46	44	50
Middlesbrough	38	11	10	17	35	50	43
Leeds United	38	12	7	19	40	57	43
Wimbledon	38	10	11	17	55	70	41
Sheffield Wednesday	38	10	10	18	48	61	40
Coventry City	38	8	14	16	42	60	38
Southampton	38	9	11	18	34	52	38
Manchester City	**38**	**9**	**11**	**18**	**33**	**58**	**38**
Queen's Pk. Rangers	38	9	6	23	38	57	33
Bolton Wanderers	38	8	5	25	39	71	29

1996-97 SEASON

FIRST DIVISION

Bolton Wanderers	46	28	14	4	100	53	98
Barnsley	46	22	14	10	76	55	80
Wolverhampton Wns.	46	22	10	14	68	51	76
Ipswich Town	46	20	14	12	68	50	74
Sheffield United	46	20	13	13	75	52	73
Crystal Palace	46	19	14	13	78	48	71
Portsmouth	46	20	8	18	59	53	68
Port Vale	46	17	16	13	58	55	67
Queen's Pk. Rangers	46	18	12	16	64	60	66
Birmingham City	46	17	15	14	52	48	66
Tranmere Rovers	46	17	14	15	63	56	65
Stoke City	46	18	10	18	51	57	64
Norwich City	46	17	12	17	63	68	63
Manchester City	**46**	**17**	**10**	**19**	**59**	**60**	**61**
Charlton Athletic	46	16	11	19	52	66	59
West Brom. Albion	46	14	15	17	68	72	57
Oxford United	46	16	9	21	64	68	57
Reading	46	15	12	19	58	67	57
Swindon Town	46	15	9	22	52	71	54
Huddersfield Town	46	13	15	18	48	61	54
Bradford City	46	12	12	22	47	72	48
Grimsby Town	46	11	13	22	60	81	46
Oldham Athletic	46	10	13	23	51	66	43
Southend United	46	8	15	23	42	86	39

1997-98 SEASON

FIRST DIVISION

Nottingham Forest	46	28	10	8	82	42	94
Middlesbrough	46	27	10	9	77	41	91
Sunderland	46	26	12	8	86	50	90
Charlton Athletic	46	26	10	10	80	49	88
Ipswich Town	46	23	14	9	77	43	83
Sheffield United	46	19	17	10	69	54	74
Birmingham City	46	19	17	10	60	35	74
Stockport County	46	19	8	19	71	69	65
Wolverhampton Wns.	46	18	11	17	57	53	65
West Brom. Albion	46	16	13	17	50	56	61
Crewe Alexandra	46	18	5	23	58	65	59
Oxford United	46	16	10	20	60	64	58
Bradford City	46	14	15	17	46	59	57
Tranmere Rovers	46	14	14	18	54	57	56
Norwich City	46	14	13	19	52	69	55
Huddersfield Town	46	14	11	21	50	72	53
Bury	46	11	19	16	42	58	52
Swindon Town	46	14	10	22	42	73	52
Port Vale	46	13	10	23	56	66	49
Portsmouth	46	13	10	23	51	63	49
Queen's Pk. Rangers	46	10	19	17	51	63	49
Manchester City	**46**	**12**	**12**	**22**	**56**	**57**	**48**
Stoke City	46	11	13	22	44	74	46
Reading	46	11	9	26	39	78	42